THIS BOOK BELONGS TO:

____

31 Days Through Proverbs

Published by HarperChristian Resources, 3950 Sparks Drive SE, Suite 101, Grand Rapids, MI 49546, USA.
HarperChristian Resources is a registered trademark of HarperCollins Christian Publishing, Inc.

Requests for information should be sent to customercare@harpercollins.com.

ISBN 978-0-310-17868-2 (softcover)

ISBN 978-0-310-17869-9 (ebook)

HarperCollins Publishers, Macken House, 39/40 Mayor Street Upper, Dublin 1, D01 C9W8, Ireland (https://www.harpercollins.com).

Art Direction: Ron Huizinga
Cover Design: Ron Huizinga
Interior Design: Riley Goodman Moody / goodmooddesignco.com

First Printing July 2026 / Printed in the United States of America

31 DAYS THROUGH PROVERBS

WISDOM FOR EVERY DAY

PROVERBS 31 MINISTRIES

HarperChristian Resources

WELCOME LETTER

Dear friends,

When my firstborn came home from his first day of kindergarten, he shuffled through the door with sagging shoulders and a droopy frown.

"What's wrong?" I asked as he plunked his backpack on the floor and climbed up on the counter, where he sat with skinny legs dangling over the edge.

My son dropped his head into his hands and began to cry. "Mommy," he said with a jagged sigh, "I don't know if I can go to kindergarten anymore. **My head hurts from deciding too much!**"

Perhaps it's been a while since you've had to decide what crayon to use or what carpet square to sit on. But I'm guessing you know the ache of **decision fatigue** too. Our days can feel like an endless string of choices to be made and options to be weighed. Eventually, all the culling and considering, speculating and navigating, can make our brains hurt and our hearts feel weary.

Are the countless decisions adding up to a life that counts? Are we living our one life well?

The book of Proverbs was written to help us answer these questions. Different from other books of the Bible, Proverbs doesn't spend a lot of words on deep theology or intricate ideology. It doesn't primarily recite religious law or historical facts. Instead, it's filled with practical instruction to help us develop a set of skills for living well in God's world.[1] It gives wisdom for our steps and encouragement for our anxious hearts. As one scholar says, "While other parts of Scripture show us the glory of our high calling, the Book of Proverbs instructs us in detail how we should walk so that we are worthy of this calling."[2]

For the next 31 days, we'll explore this unique book and discover what it means to apply wisdom to the ups and downs of our daily lives. We'll glean insight on managing money and stewarding time, serving our families and settling disagreements. We'll discover how Proverbs guides us in practical and helpful ways when we're tired and angry, confused and conflicted.

This study will equip you to navigate daily challenges and circumstances more confidently. Seeking guidance for everyday decision-making in Scripture will always lead you to God's best for your life. *"For the LORD gives wisdom; from his mouth come knowledge and understanding"* (Proverbs 2:6).

Come as you are. Bring your hurting head, your weary feet, and your humble heart. Bring your questions and your quandaries, your worries and your hopes.

We won't sit on carpet squares, but we'll gather around God's Word. And together, we'll discover how to live this one life well.

Welcome to Proverbs!

Alicia Bruxvoort and Claire Foxx
Co-authors

How and to Where Our Decisions Lead Us

JESUS IS THE WAY

"Two roads diverged in a yellow wood
And sorry I could not travel both
And be one traveler, long I stood . . ."[1]

So begins Robert Frost's famous poem about decision-making, titled "The Road Not Taken." Interestingly, similar crossroads imagery shows up throughout the book of Proverbs, which uses the words *path* (23 times) and *way* (76 times) more than any other book of the Bible, frequently contrasting the route of righteousness and the route of wickedness. One of the main themes in Proverbs is that we all get to choose which of these two roads we will travel.

But of course, life often doesn't seem as straightforward as that. **Studies estimate that most modern adults make about 35,000 conscious choices every day.** It's no wonder we question if it's even possible to practice moment-by-moment thoughtfulness in a world asking us to make a decision about every 30 seconds![2]

What if one single decision actually helps us solve this problem?

Pastor David Murray observes that when we read Proverbs through a gospel (or Jesus-centered) lens, we discover that instead of thousands of choices to ponder, Proverbs offers really just one: "a choice between two people. It's a choice between a person who is folly (the devil) and a person who is wise (the Son of God)."[3]

Proverbs cuts through all the clutter to the heart of why our daily decisions really matter: They lead us either toward God or away from Him.

And when we think about it this way, we come to understand that *what* we choose every day is important—but most important is *whom* we choose.

The way to live a wise and righteous life filled with the fruit of good decisions isn't an equation for calculating opportunity costs. The way isn't a 21-day challenge for forming good habits. The way isn't better time management or a well-written pro/con list.

Jesus said, ***"I am the way*** *and the truth and the life"* (John 14:6, emphasis added).

So no matter what kind of crossroads we face today, the right path to take is the one with Jesus' footprints on it.

His way is humility and hope. His way is surrender and salvation. It's not always the easiest way—after all, it led Him to the cross—but it is the way of love and abundant life forever with God.

When we carefully ponder the gospel of Jesus' life, death, and resurrection and choose to trust in Him wholeheartedly, day after day, we will find that our other 34,999 choices tend to work themselves out. He truly makes all the difference.

What Are Proverbs?

HOW SHOULD WE READ THEM?

The book of Proverbs is an anthology of precious, time-honored guidance God gave us, His people.

Before we jump into studying Proverbs up close, let's zoom out to consider the overall genre and purpose of this book and how to apply it to our lives as part of God's Word.

GENRE & DESCRIPTION	PURPOSE
Wisdom Literature • Practical sayings passed down through oral tradition • Bite-sized ancient wisdom • Principles for living righteously	Make the complex simple Make the abstract concrete Guidebook for how to become more like Jesus—faithfully pursuing God's will in every decision

We can thank God that the book of Proverbs is extremely applicable to our lives. Even children can understand the basic meaning of most proverbs; in fact, some are addressed to children or young men. Proverbs confirms there is an ideal "*way [we] should go*" (Proverbs 22:6)—God's way. However, Proverbs does not promise that God's people will always have ideal experiences in every situation on this side of eternity. The assurances in Proverbs may sound to us like guarantees of favorable earthly outcomes, yet because our world is tainted by sin, even someone who perfectly obeyed the wisdom principles in Proverbs might still face strife, sorrow, and struggles in this life. We know this because someone *has* perfectly obeyed. His name is Jesus. He lived as "*a man of sorrows and acquainted with grief*" (Isaiah 53:3 ESV).

So in the end, if we try to read Proverbs as a guidebook for how to become successful, prosperous, and problem-free through righteous decision-making, we may find ourselves ultimately disappointed. But if we read it as a guidebook for how to become **more like Christ**—faithfully pursuing God's will in every decision we make, even when our current circumstances are less than ideal—we will find it is indeed *"much better to get wisdom than gold"* or any earthly reward (Proverbs 16:16).

Who Wrote Proverbs?

Before they were written and preserved in the Bible, many of the wisdom sayings found in Proverbs were exactly that—sayings, passed down through oral tradition among generations of ancient Israelites whose perspectives on life were shaped by their experiences of God's redemption and revelation. Imagine sitting around a campfire and hearing your parents, grandparents, or great-grandparents share powerful stories to impart God-inspired wisdom they learned from *their* parents and grandparents. The book of Proverbs is an anthology of this type of precious, time-honored guidance God gave His people.

Many scholars believe the Scriptures that make up Proverbs were compiled primarily during the reign of King Solomon (around 971–931 BC). Different parts of the book may have been written at different times.

Though some scholars believe Proverbs should be attributed solely to King Solomon, most theorize there were at least three authors—Solomon, Agur, and Lemuel—whose writings were compiled by editors to form the book of Proverbs.

In terms of organization, Proverbs can be divided into four parts:

THE BOOK OF SOLOMON	HEZEKIAH	THE SAYINGS OF AGUR	THE SAYINGS OF LEMUEL
CHAPTERS 1-24	CHAPTERS 25-29	CHAPTER 30	CHAPTER 31

CHAPTERS 1-9	DISCOURSE, OR A SET OF SPEECHES ABOUT WISDOM
CHAPTERS 10-22	TRADITIONAL PROVERBS
CHAPTERS 22-24	"SAYINGS": UNITS OF WISDOM THAT MAKE UP SEVERAL VERSES[1]

WHO WAS KING SOLOMON?

King Solomon is widely known as the wisest king ever to live. He was the son of King David and Bathsheba (2 Samuel 12:24–25) and ruled as the third king of Israel. Solomon was the last king to rule a united Israel prior to its division into the northern and southern kingdoms. We can read about Solomon's reign in 1 Kings 2–11.

Solomon achieved tremendous successes as king, like building the temple in Jerusalem and establishing political alliances for Israel. His most notable and necessary asset in achieving this success was the wisdom God gave him in 1 Kings 3:4–15. God offered to give Solomon whatever he asked for, and Solomon requested *"an understanding mind to govern your people, that I may discern between good and evil"* (1 Kings 3:9 ESV).

In the end, Solomon wasn't perfect, and he still fell prey to sin as his heart turned toward the gods of his many pagan wives (1 Kings 11:4). Thankfully, today we have *"something greater than Solomon"* in our perfect Savior, King Jesus (Matthew 12:42)!

WHO WAS AGUR?

Agur is mentioned as the author of Proverbs 30, but he is never mentioned anywhere else in Scripture. Some scholars believe his name means "gatherer," so Agur can be seen as someone who gathered wisdom. The fact that we don't know a lot about Agur is actually encouraging for believers today. God can and will make much of Himself through the faithfulness of the humble.

WHO WAS LEMUEL?

King Lemuel is referenced as the author of Proverbs 31:1–9 (which is also described as *"an oracle that his mother taught him"* [v. 1 ESV]). Scholars believe it's possible that Lemuel is associated with Massa, the seventh son of Ishmael, which would connect King Lemuel to Israel's patriarch Abraham (Genesis 16:15; Genesis 25:13–14). The name *Lemuel* in Hebrew means "for God" or "devoted to God."

MAJOR THEMES IN PROVERBS

As we read through Proverbs, we can be encouraged that these 31 chapters cover a wide array of situations, possibilities, and dilemmas of the human experience—in other words, the things we make decisions about every day. The variety of topics in Proverbs reminds us there is not a single aspect of life where we cannot benefit from knowing how to make godly decisions.

ANGER	Proverbs 12:16; 14:17; 14:29; 15:1; 15:18; 16:32; 19:3; 19:11; 19:19; 20:2; 21:14; 22:24–25; 29:22
CHILDREN	Proverbs 10:1; 13:1; 13:24; 14:26; 15:20; 17:6; 17:21; 17:25; 19:13; 19:18; 19:26; 20:11; 20:20; 22:6; 22:15; 23:13–14; 23:22–25; 28:7; 28:24; 29:15; 29:17
CONTENTMENT	Proverbs 13:25; 14:30; 16:8; 19:23; 23:4–5; 25:16; 30:15–16
COURAGE	Proverbs 24:10–12; 25:26; 28:1
DEBT	Proverbs 6:1–5; 17:18; 20:16; 22:7; 22:26–27; 27:13
DISHONESTY	Proverbs 6:16–19; 10:18; 11:1; 12:17; 12:19; 12:22; 13:5; 14:5; 14:25; 16:28; 16:30; 17:7; 17:20; 19:5; 19:9; 19:22; 20:10; 20:14; 20:17; 20:23; 21:6; 21:28; 24:28–29; 25:14; 25:18; 26:18–19; 26:23–28; 29:12; 30:8
ENVY	Proverbs 3:31–32; 12:12; 14:30; 23:17–18; 24:1–2; 24:19–20
FOOLISHNESS	Proverbs 1:32–33; 9:13–18; 11:29; 12:15; 12:23; 13:16; 14:1; 14:7; 14:8; 14:16; 14:18; 14:24; 14:29; 15:2; 15:5; 15:14; 15:21; 17:10; 17:12; 18:2; 18:13; 20:3; 24:8–9; 26:4–5; 26:11; 27:22; 28:26; 29:9; 29:11

FRIENDS	Proverbs 13:20; 14:20; 16:28; 17:9; 17:17; 18:24; 19:4; 19:6; 19:7; 20:6; 20:19; 22:24–25; 27:6; 27:9; 27:10; 27:17
GENEROSITY	Proverbs 11:24; 11:25; 14:21; 14:31; 19:6; 19:17; 21:25-26; 22:9; 25:21–22; 28:8; 28:27; 31:20
GOVERNMENT	Proverbs 8:15–16; 14:28; 16:10; 16:12; 16:14–15; 19:12; 20:2; 20:8; 20:26; 20:28; 21:1; 24:21–22; 25:1–7; 28:2; 28:12; 28:15–16; 29:2; 29:4; 29:12; 29:14; 29:26; 31:4–9
GREED	Proverbs 1:10–19; 11:26; 12:12; 13:11; 15:27; 17:23; 20:21; 21:13; 21:25–26; 22:16; 22:28; 23:10–11; 27:20; 28:8; 28:20; 28:22; 28:25; 29:4; 30:15–16
HONESTY	Proverbs 4:24; 11:1; 12:17; 12:19; 14:5; 14:25; 16:11; 16:13; 24:26; 27:5; 28:13; 28:23
HUMILITY	Proverbs 11:2; 12:9; 12:15; 13:13; 15:33; 16:19; 18:12; 22:4; 25:6-7; 25:27; 27:2; 29:23
INJUSTICE	Proverbs 1:19; 13:23; 15:27; 16:8; 17:15; 17:23; 18:5; 21:7; 22:8; 22:16; 24:23–25; 28:16; 28:21; 29:27
JUSTICE	Proverbs 2:6–8; 11:1; 12:5; 16:10; 16:11; 19:28; 20:8; 21:3; 21:15; 22:22–23; 28:5; 29:4; 29:14; 29:26; 31:9
LAZINESS	Proverbs 6:6-11; 10:4; 10:5; 10:26; 12:11; 12:24; 12:27; 13:4; 14:23; 15:19; 18:9; 19:15; 19:24; 20:4; 20:13; 21:25-26; 22:13; 24:30–34; 26:13; 26:14; 26:15; 26:16
MARRIAGE	Proverbs 5:15–19; 15:17; 18:22; 19:13; 21:9; 21:19; 27:15-16; 30:21-23; 31:10–11

NEIGHBORS	Proverbs 3:28; 11:9; 11:12; 14:20; 14:21; 16:29; 21:10; 24:28–29; 25:8–10; 25:17; 25:18; 26:18–19; 27:14; 29:5
PATIENCE	Proverbs 13:11; 14:29; 15:18; 16:32; 19:2; 19:11; 20:22; 20:25; 21:5; 25:15; 28:20; 29:20
POVERTY	Proverbs 6:10–11; 10:4; 10:15; 13:7; 13:8; 13:23; 14:20; 14:23; 14:31; 15:16; 16:8; 16:19; 17:5; 18:23; 19:1; 19:4; 19:7; 19:17; 20:13; 21:5; 21:13; 21:17; 22:2; 22:7; 22:16; 22:22–23; 23:10–11; 23:20–21; 28:3; 28:6; 28:19; 29:7
PRIDE	Proverbs 8:13; 11:2; 12:9; 12:15; 15:12; 15:25; 15:32; 16:5; 16:18; 16:19; 18:12; 21:4; 21:24; 25:27; 26:12; 26:16; 27:1; 29:1; 29:23; 30:11–14
SEXUAL IMMORALITY	Proverbs 5:1–23; 6:20–7:27; 22:14; 23:26–28; 29:3
WEALTH	Proverbs 10:4; 10:15; 13:7; 13:8; 13:18; 14:20; 15:16; 16:8; 16:19; 18:23; 19:4; 22:2; 22:7; 28:6; 28:8; 28:11
WORK	Proverbs 6:6–11; 10:4; 10:5; 12:11; 12:14; 12:24; 12:27; 13:4; 14:23; 16:26; 18:9; 20:13; 21:5; 22:29; 23:4–5; 24:27; 24:30–34; 26:10; 28:19; 31:27

What You Have to Look Forward to in This Study

DAILY TEACHINGS AND REFLECTION QUESTIONS

Each day of this study we will unwrap a chapter of Proverbs together and learn how to apply these Scriptures to our daily lives and decisions. You'll find reflection questions throughout to guide your personal study.

BONUS PAGES

Sprinkled throughout this guide, you'll also find some special charts, topical mini-studies, explanations of tricky verses, frameworks for biblical decision-making, and more!

TABLE OF

CONTENTS

DAY 1

PROVERBS 1

The Fear of God Is the Beginning of Wise Decisions

Let's get started! Though the book of Proverbs was written by multiple writers, Proverbs 1:1 reads like a byline with just one name: *Solomon*. First Kings 3:12 hails him as the wisest man to ever live. Before we move forward, let's take a quick glance back and discover where Solomon gained his iconic acumen.

Read 1 Kings 3:5–12. What (or who) was Solomon most concerned with?

What are a few key concerns Solomon had in response to God's incredible statement that you can hold on to as you begin learning new ways to make better decisions?

Read 1 Kings 4:29–31. First Kings 4:29 begins like this: *"And God gave Solomon . . ."* Do you see the good news in those four little words? They remind us wisdom isn't a product of personal greatness or elite scholarship; it's simply a gift from our great and gracious God. What does this reveal to you about God's desire for your priorities and motives?

READ AND RESPOND

PROVERBS 1

1 The proverbs of Solomon son of David, king of Israel:

2 for gaining wisdom and instruction;
for understanding words of insight;
3 for receiving instruction in prudent behavior,
doing what is right and just and fair;
4 for giving prudence to those who are simple,
knowledge and discretion to the young—
5 let the wise listen and add to their learning,
and let the discerning get guidance—
6 for understanding proverbs and parables,
the sayings and riddles of the wise.

7 The fear of the LORD is the beginning of knowledge,
but fools despise wisdom and instruction.

Prologue: Exhortations to Embrace Wisdom

WARNING AGAINST THE INVITATION OF SINFUL MEN

8 Listen, my son, to your father's instruction
and do not forsake your mother's teaching.
9 They are a garland to grace your head
and a chain to adorn your neck.

10 My son, if sinful men entice you,
do not give in to them.
11 If they say, "Come along with us;
let's lie in wait for innocent blood,
let's ambush some harmless soul;
12 let's swallow them alive, like the grave,
and whole, like those who go down to the pit;
13 we will get all sorts of valuable things
and fill our houses with plunder;
14 cast lots with us;
we will all share the loot"—
15 my son, do not go along with them,
do not set foot on their paths;
16 for their feet rush into evil,
they are swift to shed blood.
17 How useless to spread a net

where every bird can see it!
18 These men lie in wait
for their own blood;
they ambush only themselves!
19 Such are the paths of all who
go after ill-gotten gain;
it takes away the life of those who get it.

WISDOM'S REBUKE

20 Out in the open wisdom calls aloud,
she raises her voice in the public square;
21 on top of the wall she cries out,
at the city gate she makes her speech:

22 "How long will you who are sim-
ple love your simple ways?
How long will mock-
ers delight in mockery
and fools hate knowledge?
23 Repent at my rebuke!
Then I will pour out my
thoughts to you,
I will make known to you my teachings.
24 But since you refuse to lis-
ten when I call
and no one pays attention
when I stretch out my hand,
25 since you disregard all my advice
and do not accept my rebuke,
26 I in turn will laugh when di-
saster strikes you;
I will mock when calam-
ity overtakes you—
27 when calamity over-
takes you like a storm,
when disaster sweeps over
you like a whirlwind,
when distress and trou-
ble overwhelm you.

28 "Then they will call to me
but I will not answer;
they will look for me but
will not find me,
29 since they hated knowledge
and did not choose to fear the LORD.
30 Since they would not accept my advice
and spurned my rebuke,
31 they will eat the fruit of their ways
and be filled with the
fruit of their schemes.
32 For the waywardness of the
simple will kill them,
and the complacency of
fools will destroy them;
33 but whoever listens to
me will live in safety
and be at ease, without fear of harm."

The source of Solomon's wisdom is the source of our wisdom too. Circle Proverbs 1:7. Underline the phrases in verses 2–6 that describe what these proverbs are for.

What must our pursuit of wisdom be rooted in?

What comes to mind when you hear the phrase *"the fear of the LORD"*?

We often associate fear with the notion of being scared or shaken. Or sometimes we see fear of the Lord as meaning simply having some respect. But neither of these is the intended meaning of this ancient idiom. In the original Hebrew, יְהוָה יִרְאָה *Yirah Yhvh*, this little phrase carries the ideas of *awe*, *worship*, *obedience*, *reverence*, and *trust*.

This concept in Proverbs 1:7 is so important Solomon mentioned it again, word for word, in Proverbs 9:10. Ultimately, he wanted us to understand that wisdom doesn't just start with right thinking; it begins with a right-sized view of God.

What sense do you get of the parent-to-child communication in verses 8–19?

LOVING — CARING — PROTECTIVE — PUNITIVE — DISTANT

Author A. W. Tozer suggests, "What comes into our minds when we think about God is the most important thing about us."[1] Write down some of the words or images that come to mind when you think of God.

Now read your list on the previous page, and circle the words that make you want to draw near to God.

Next, put an X beside the words that make you want to avoid God. Before we go any further, let's ask God to use this study to reveal any misconceptions we have of Him and to show us more of who He really is.

Read verses 20–33. What stands out to you in these last verses?

Proverbs 1:20–33 closes with a poetic picture of Lady Wisdom crying out in the middle of the marketplace. The marketplace in ancient Israel was more than just an ancient mall—it was the hub of daily life. A place for assembly and open discussion, social connection and commerce, the marketplace was filled with rowdy debates and friendly chatter, the singsong of vendors and the laughter of children.

This setting communicates the practicality and accessibility of God's wisdom. We don't need to be in a classroom, courthouse, church, or library to receive it. We can find it in the ebb and flow of the everyday—right where our daily needs intersect with God's generous heart.

Read Proverbs 1:23 once again and relish the reminder that God's insight is available to you. As we continue through Proverbs, be on the lookout for practical guidance that speaks to your specific situation.

DAY 2

PROVERBS 2

My Role in Choosing Wisdom

Have you heard of the Copper Scroll? That's the name of the earliest known treasure map. Recovered among the Dead Sea Scrolls in 1952, this document, composed of copper rather than parchment, lists sixty-three locations with detailed instructions on how to recover a vast treasure hidden throughout the Judean wilderness.[1]

Of course, we don't need an ancient map to hunt for precious bounty. The second chapter of Proverbs points us to priceless treasure too. As this chapter begins, Solomon assumes the instructive voice of a father and urges us to recognize wisdom's immeasurable worth and prioritize our pursuit of it.

What are the things you treasure most in your life? Write them in the treasure box below. Keep these things in mind as we explore Proverbs 2.

READ AND RESPOND

PROVERBS 2

1 My son, if you accept my words
and store up my commands within you,
2 turning your ear to wisdom
and applying your heart
to understanding—
3 indeed, if you call out for insight
and cry aloud for understanding,
4 and if you look for it as for silver
and search for it as for hidden treasure,
5 then you will understand
the fear of the LORD
and find the knowledge of God.
6 For the LORD gives wisdom;
from his mouth come knowl-
edge and understanding.
7 He holds success in store for the upright,
he is a shield to those
whose walk is blameless,
8 for he guards the course of the just
and protects the way of
his faithful ones.

9 Then you will understand
what is right and just
and fair—every good path.
10 For wisdom will enter your heart,
and knowledge will be
pleasant to your soul.
11 Discretion will protect you,
and understanding will guard you.

12 Wisdom will save you from
the ways of wicked men,
from men whose words are perverse,
13 who have left the straight paths
to walk in dark ways,
14 who delight in doing wrong
and rejoice in the perverseness of evil,
15 whose paths are crooked
and who are devious in their ways.

16 Wisdom will save you also
from the adulterous woman,
from the wayward woman
with her seductive words,
17 who has left the partner of her youth
and ignored the covenant
she made before God.
18 Surely her house leads down to death
and her paths to the spirits of the dead.
19 None who go to her return
or attain the paths of life.

20 Thus you will walk in

the ways of the good
and keep to the paths of the righteous.
21 For the upright will live in the land,
and the blameless will remain in it;
22 but the wicked will be
cut off from the land,
and the unfaithful will be torn from it.

Read verses 1–5 of Proverbs 2 in light of how wisdom is described in Proverbs 1:20–23. Make a short list of the ways we benefit from listening to wisdom:

The tone might make you feel like you're a soldier receiving marching orders. These verses read like an urgent call to action and remind us we have an important role to play in the treasure hunt for wisdom.

Look up and read Matthew 7:7–8. What do Jesus' words in Matthew have in common with Solomon's words in Proverbs 2:1–9?

If we're honest, life can feel like a constant clatter. Jobs, struggles, relationships, obligations, and even the phones in our pockets vie for our attention. Sometimes we need to pause and sift through it all to make sure we can still hear wisdom's call.

Make a list of ten things that call out for your attention each day. Now rank those things in order of priority.

Compare the words on your list to the words in your treasure box. Are you spending your time on what you treasure? Why or why not?

Proverbs 2 doesn't diminish the demands of daily life; it simply highlights the incomparable value of spending time with God (vv. 6–11, 20), and it challenges us to allocate our time and attention accordingly. We may need to change our habits if we want God's Word to change our hearts!

Read Proverbs 2 again and highlight, underline, or circle the rewards of treasuring God's Word and seeking wisdom.

We aren't called to a passive experience with God's Word but an active one. The Hebrew word for "receive" in verse 1 is *laqach*, which means "to seize, to capture, to take and carry away."

laqach (לָקַח)

TO SEIZE, TO CAPTURE, TO TAKE AND CARRY AWAY

As we mine the truths of Scripture, we don't just encounter slivers of history and strands of advice, we *"find the knowledge of God"* (v. 5) spoken directly from His own mouth (v. 6). And the more we know Him, the more we're able to see life from His perspective (v. 9) in every daily circumstance.

BE COMMITTED TO PRACTICE WISDOM

LYSA TERKEURST

Wisdom is a gift from God, but it's a gift that must be utilized by us. A life of wisdom is something we diligently seek after and purposefully live out. Simply put, living a godly life takes effort on our part.

This reminds me of when my family adopted our two sons, Jackson and Mark. When we brought them home to the United States, they were thirteen and fourteen years old. But when we had them evaluated for school, we realized they would need to do some catching up to join their peers in eighth grade. There really was no other option but for me to homeschool them.

I was completely overwhelmed at the assignment before me. But instead of trying to do it perfectly, I decided just to do it willingly. I never became a great teacher, but God honored my willingness to simply show up. My sons and I sat at our farmhouse table many days feeling frustrated. But together, morning after morning, we stayed the course. And I'm so grateful we did. In just two short years, they made tremendous progress and eventually were ready to go to school on their own.

No matter what, we were committed. And the same must be true for all of us if we want to make godly decisions. If we want the wisdom to know what to do when it matters most, we've got to be committed to show up and practice wisdom daily.

Proverbs 2:1–4 gives us clear instruction on the way to access wisdom, use wisdom, and be protected by wisdom:

1. Receive God's Word (Proverbs 2:1). God's Word is a gift. But our responsibility is to receive the gift, open the gift, and use the gift.

2. Treasure up His commands within us (Proverbs 2:1). We are to get into God's Word and let God's Word get into us. The more verses we memorize and live out, the more our thinking will align with His Truth.

3. Make our ears attentive to wisdom (Proverbs 2:2). We can do this by listening to wise teaching and advice and keeping the company of wise people (Proverbs 13:20; Proverbs 2:20).

4. Call out for insight (Proverbs 2:3). Today, as believers in Jesus, we can ask the Holy Spirit who dwells in us (Romans 8:11; John 14:26) to open our eyes and to show us wondrous things in God's Word (Psalm 119:18; Psalm 119:130).

5. Ask for understanding (Proverbs 2:3). We cry out to the Lord for understanding not just for academic purposes but for the purpose of spiritual growth and maturity.

6. Search for wisdom as passionately as we would hunt for hidden treasure (Proverbs 2:4). Wisdom comes from the Lord, and the value of His wisdom is higher than that of anything the world offers.

I don't want us to miss out on the protection that comes from living according to God's Word and His ways. Proverbs 2:11–12 (ESV) gives us such a vivid picture of how wisdom serves as a moral safeguard: *"Discretion will watch over you, understanding will guard you, delivering you from the way of evil. . . ."* When we allow godly wisdom to direct our way of thinking, thoughts of depravity will become more and more foreign to us. We'll be better equipped to recognize and avoid the snares of the enemy. We'll be empowered to make decisions today that will still be good tomorrow.

But to be wise decision-makers, we have to put our hearts and our minds in places where wisdom gathers, not scatters.

Wisdom gathers in your Bible study group. Wisdom gathers where you serve and invest in your local church. Wisdom gathers in conversations that are God-honoring.

Let's ask God to help us take an honest look at where we have been parking our hearts and our minds lately. Are they gathering places or scattering places?

DAY 3

PROVERBS 3

How to Avoid Regret

It seemed like a good idea at the time . . . .

How many times have you stood on the other side of a decision and muttered those words with a shrug of disbelief or a sigh of regret?

We've all made choices that, in retrospect, we'd choose to change. That's why Proverbs 3 reminds us that navigating life using only our own ideas isn't the best idea. God's ideas, specifically the directives found in His Word, are a more trustworthy guide.

> When was the last time you made a decision that left you wishing for a do-over? How did the outcome of that decision leave you feeling?

READ AND RESPOND

PROVERBS 3

1 My son, do not forget my teaching,
but keep my commands in your heart,
2 for they will prolong your life many years
and bring you peace and prosperity.

3 Let love and faithful-
ness never leave you;
bind them around your neck,
write them on the tablet of your heart.
4 Then you will win fa-
vor and a good name
in the sight of God and man.

5 Trust in the LORD with all your heart
and lean not on your
own understanding;
6 in all your ways submit to him,
and he will make your paths straight.

7 Do not be wise in your own eyes;

fear the LORD and shun evil.
8 This will bring health to your body
and nourishment to your bones.

9 Honor the LORD with your wealth,
with the firstfruits of all your crops;
10 then your barns will be
filled to overflowing,
and your vats will brim
over with new wine.

11 My son, do not despise
the LORD's discipline,
and do not resent his rebuke,
12 because the LORD disci-
plines those he loves,
as a father the son he delights in.

13 Blessed are those who find wisdom,
those who gain understanding,
14 for she is more profitable than silver
and yields better returns than gold.
15 She is more precious than rubies;
nothing you desire can
compare with her.
16 Long life is in her right hand;
in her left hand are riches and honor.
17 Her ways are pleasant ways,
and all her paths are peace.
18 She is a tree of life to those
who take hold of her;
those who hold her fast will be blessed.

19 By wisdom the LORD laid
the earth's foundations,
by understanding he set
the heavens in place;
20 by his knowledge the wa-
tery depths were divided,
and the clouds let drop the dew.

21 My son, do not let wisdom and
understanding out of your sight,
preserve sound judg-
ment and discretion;
22 they will be life for you,
an ornament to grace your neck.
23 Then you will go on your way in safety,
and your foot will not stumble.
24 When you lie down, you
will not be afraid;
when you lie down, your
sleep will be sweet.
25 Have no fear of sudden disaster
or of the ruin that overtakes the wicked,
26 for the LORD will be at your side
and will keep your foot
from being snared.

27 Do not withhold good from

those to whom it is due,
when it is in your power to act.
28 Do not say to your neighbor,
"Come back tomorrow and
I'll give it to you"—
when you already have it with you.
29 Do not plot harm against
your neighbor,
who lives trustfully near you.
30 Do not accuse anyone for no reason—
when they have done you no harm.

31 Do not envy the violent
or choose any of their ways.
32 For the LORD detests the perverse
but takes the upright
into his confidence.
33 The LORD's curse is on the
house of the wicked,
but he blesses the home
of the righteous.
34 He mocks proud mockers
but shows favor to the hum-
ble and oppressed.
35 The wise inherit honor,
but fools get only shame.

What does Proverbs 3:2 promise as a result of aligning our decisions with God's Word?

Much of Proverbs 3 is written as a series of recommendations paired with results. These imperative statements follow a simple pattern: If you do (or don't do) *this*, the result will be *that*.

Scan through the chapter, and list some of the pairings you see. (For example, verses 1 and 2 are paired below.)

RECOMMENDATION	RESULT
Do not forget God's teaching and keep His commands in your heart (v. 1).	Life will be prolonged many years and bring peace and prosperity (v. 2).

As you glance through the pairings, it's essential to remember that many of the results refer to spiritual or moral benefits rather than physical ones. The word *peace* in verse 2 refers to wholeness, internal and external contentment, peace with God, and peace with humankind. The Hebrew word for *life* could also be translated "fullness of life." These words paint a picture of meaningful abundance.

Interestingly, Jesus echoed this idea when He announced in John 10:10b, "*I came that they may have life and have it abundantly*" (ESV).

Have you ever thought about the way God's Word adds value to your life? Take a moment to think about this: God created us with a craving for a meaningful life, and then He gave us a way to satisfy that hunger. What a good God we have!

As we move through the chapter, we see a shift in Proverbs 3:5–12 from the concept of obedience to trust. The phrases *all your heart* (v. 5) and *all your ways* (v. 6) call us to place our complete confidence in God's ways over our own.

> What makes it difficult for you to trust God with *all* your heart and in *all* your ways?

Let's admit that one of the things that makes it so hard to trust God is that He just doesn't do things like we would (Isaiah 55:8–9). He seems to move slower, take the long way around, and even define "good" quite differently than we do. But Proverbs 3 isn't advocating blind trust in God.

> Think of what you know about God's character—from His Word and your personal experience—and finish the bolded sentence below. (If you need some help, check out these verses: Numbers 23:19; Psalm 18:30; Psalm 116:5; Psalm 145:9; Isaiah 40:28; Ephesians 2:4–5; and 1 John 1:5.)
>
> **I can trust God because He is ...**

God's ways aren't haphazard. They don't hinge on His mood or change with time. They are rooted in His fathomless knowledge and eternal goodness. Best of all, the same God who dictates the rhythms of this spinning globe is willing to direct your daily path . . . if you'll trust Him.

Take a moment and thank God for that. Then step outside and let the wonder of the world around you buoy your confidence in the God who created it.

PROVERBS 4

Help from Others

Today's reading is wrapped in the faint scent of nostalgia as Solomon remembered the lessons his father, King David, taught him. By linking three generations (David, Solomon, and Solomon's son), Proverbs 4 demonstrates that we are more prone to listen to wisdom from someone to whom we're connected by friendship or family bonds, empathy or love.

Most scholars agree the phrase *my son* (Proverbs 4:10; Proverbs 4:20) is a general term applied to anyone younger in years or experience. Likewise, the father represents an older and wiser member of the community.

> Name someone you know who has godly wisdom to share. How can you be more intentional about learning from this person?

Even with those closest to us, we might sometimes feel awkward or unsure about opening up about what

READ AND RESPOND

PROVERBS 4

1 Listen, my sons, to a father's instruction;
pay attention and gain understanding.
2 I give you sound learning,
so do not forsake my teaching.
3 For I too was a son to my father,
still tender, and cherished by my mother.
4 Then he taught me, and he said to me,
"Take hold of my words with all your heart;
keep my commands, and you will live.
5 Get wisdom, get understanding;
do not forget my words or turn away from them.
6 Do not forsake wisdom, and

she will protect you;
love her, and she will watch over you.
7 The beginning of wisdom
is this: Get wisdom.
Though it cost all you have,
get understanding.
8 Cherish her, and she will exalt you;
embrace her, and she will honor you.
9 She will give you a gar-
land to grace your head
and present you with
a glorious crown."

10 Listen, my son, accept what I say,
and the years of your life will be many.
11 I instruct you in the way of wisdom
and lead you along straight paths.
12 When you walk, your steps
will not be hampered;
when you run, you will not stumble.
13 Hold on to instruc-
tion, do not let it go;
guard it well, for it is your life.
14 Do not set foot on the
path of the wicked
or walk in the way of evildoers.
15 Avoid it, do not travel on it;
turn from it and go on your way.
16 For they cannot rest until they do evil;
they are robbed of sleep till
they make someone stumble.
17 They eat the bread of wickedness
and drink the wine of violence.

18 The path of the righteous
is like the morning sun,
shining ever brighter till
the full light of day.
19 But the way of the
wicked is like deep darkness;
they do not know what
makes them stumble.

20 My son, pay attention to what I say;
turn your ear to my words.
21 Do not let them out of your sight,
keep them within your heart;
22 for they are life to those who find them
and health to one's whole body.
23 Above all else, guard your heart,
for everything you do flows from it.
24 Keep your mouth free of perversity;
keep corrupt talk far from your lips.
25 Let your eyes look straight ahead;
fix your gaze directly before you.
26 Give careful thought to
the paths for your feet
and be steadfast in all your ways.
27 Do not turn to the right or the left;
keep your foot from evil.

we've learned from God. But the Bible invites us to a casual, everyday approach to sharing wisdom:

> Impress them on your children. Talk about them when you sit at home and when you walk along the road, when you lie down and when you get up.
>
> DEUTERONOMY 6:7

What's one thing God's been teaching you lately that you can share with someone this week? Ask God for courage and opportunity to have that conversation.

Read verses 10–11. Solomon's father didn't merely lecture. He led by example. If our lives don't demonstrate the wisdom we're sharing, people may hear our words, but they likely won't heed them.

Jesus modeled this kind of instruction perfectly. He didn't just talk about God's ways; He demonstrated them with His life.

Read John 13:1–15. What wisdom was Jesus passing on to His disciples? How did His actions align with His words?

Reflecting on the truths in Proverbs 4 or other Scriptures you treasure, how does your life pass that message on to others?

As David taught his son about the art of wise living, he presented life in terms of two choices. We can choose to walk the path of the righteous or the path of the wicked (vv. 11, 14).

Fill in the chart based on verses 11–19:

WHAT ARE THE BENEFITS OF THE WAY OF WISDOM?	WHAT ARE THE CONSEQUENCES OF THE WAY OF WICKEDNESS?

According to verses 20–27, what does Solomon say are the ways to wise living?

Which does Solomon say is the most important (hint: 4:23)? Write the verse out here:

How might you take this advice and priority from Solomon and apply it to your decision-making process today?

Chapter 4 ends much the way it began, with a call to pay attention (vv. 1, 20). The repetitive nature of this appeal reminds us that if we're willing to listen and learn, wisdom always has something to teach us (vv. 20–22).

DAY 5

PROVERBS 5

Wisdom in Covenant Relationships

Today's chapter begins, *"My son, pay attention . . ."* (Proverbs 5:1) and then delivers some strong words about how God calls men to keep their hearts and bodies pure and faithful in marriage.

At first review this chapter might seem exclusive for those who are married, but these Scriptures hold wisdom for everyone! Not only for husbands in ancient Israel but for all who follow God today, Proverbs 5 casts a vision for *faithfulness* both in marriage relationships and in our relationship with the Lord.

READ AND RESPOND

PROVERBS 5

1 My son, pay attention to my wisdom,
turn your ear to my words of insight,
2 that you may maintain discretion
and your lips may preserve knowledge.
3 For the lips of the adulter-
ous woman drip honey,
and her speech is smoother than oil;
4 but in the end she is bitter as gall,
sharp as a double-edged sword.
5 Her feet go down to death;
her steps lead straight to the grave.
6 She gives no thought to the way of life;
her paths wander
aimlessly, but she does not know it.

7 Now then, my sons, listen to me;
do not turn aside from what I say.
8 Keep to a path far from her,
do not go near the door of her house,
9 lest you lose your honor to others
and your dignity to one who is cruel,
10 lest strangers feast on your wealth
and your toil enrich the
house of another.
11 At the end of your life you will groan,
when your flesh and body are spent.
12 You will say, "How I hated discipline!
How my heart spurned correction!
13 I would not obey my teachers
or turn my ear to my instructors.
14 And I was soon in serious trouble
in the assembly of God's people."

15 Drink water from your own cistern,
running water from your own well.
16 Should your springs over-
flow in the streets,
your streams of water in
the public squares?
17 Let them be yours alone,
never to be shared with strangers.
18 May your fountain be blessed,
and may you rejoice in the
wife of your youth.
19 A loving doe, a graceful deer—
may her breasts satisfy you always,
may you ever be intoxi-
cated with her love.
20 Why, my son, be
intoxicated with another man's wife?
Why embrace the bosom
of a wayward woman?

21 For your ways are in full
view of the LORD,
and he examines all your paths.
22 The evil deeds of the
wicked ensnare them;
the cords of their sins hold them fast.
23 For lack of discipline they will die,
led astray by their own great folly.

Let's look at how Proverbs 5 affirms God's design for loyal, covenantal marriages between one husband and one wife, following the model He established with Adam and Eve in Genesis 2.

In verses 18–19a, Solomon told his son: *"May your ____________________ be blessed, and may you rejoice in the ________________ of your youth. A loving ______________, a graceful ________________."*

In what ways does this echo the intention of the union of a man and a woman in marriage in Genesis 2:24?

Focus on verse 19. The "her" is to be understood as the wife. Read the verse below with "her / the wife" crossed out and respond:

> *A loving doe, a graceful deer—*
> *may ~~her~~ breasts satisfy you always,*
> *may you ever be intoxicated with ~~her~~ love.*

How many ways can the male/female relationship go wrong outside of the marriage covenant?

Rank the importance of reading this Proverb in full context and with its intended meaning.

PERMISSION FOR PROMISCUITY —— COMPLETE BODILY COMMITMENT TO ONE'S WIFE

One fountain. One wife. She is lovely like one deer or one graceful doe. Clearly, faithfulness is the focus here!

But it's also important to note that these verses are more than mere "thou shalt nots" reminding us that God forbids polygamy, adultery, and sexual promiscuity. **They also remind us why God created marriage—not to hold anyone back from romantic fulfillment but to define the kind of romance He designed to fulfill both men and women.** Sexual intimacy in a faithful, biblical marriage is life-giving and delightful!

Read verses 15–16. Consider the practical nature of Solomon's analogy here. In Ancient Near East culture, "streams of water in the public square" would have been understood as wastewater from the public bathrooms.

How might you rewrite these verses to a person wrestling with decisions of fidelity or promiscuity today?

Now let's **read 1 Kings 11:1–5**. How many wives did Solomon marry? What was the result?

How does this shape your reading of Solomon's advice to his son (especially the warning in Proverbs 5:23)?

While lacking knowledge is dangerous, Solomon spoke from experience when he said *"lack of discipline"* is also life-threatening (v. 23). He *knew better* than to reject God's design for marriage—but he didn't *choose better*.[1]

And whether the temptations we face are similar to or different from Solomon's, we all live in a world that entices us to stray from our good God. He is the One who calls us His bride (Revelation 21:2; Ephesians 5:25) and who *"abound[s] in steadfast love and faithfulness"* to us (Psalm 86:15 ESV). Ultimately, marital disloyalty is just one example of how all sin is an act of disloyalty to Him.

So how do we avoid being *"led astray"* (Proverbs 5:23)? We find one practical strategy in verse 8: *"Keep your way far from her, and do not go near the door of her house"* (ESV). Once we know where temptation lives, we mark that spot on our mental map and steer clear.

> Keep your way far from her, and do not go near the door of her house.
>
> PROVERBS 5:8 (ESV)

Scan the verses one more time and write down the other practical strategies Solomon offered for decisions of sexual intimacy:

Note the verbs and verb phrases Solomon calls for in verses 1, 7, and 13. Write below how to summarize his instruction in one single word: ______________________________.

How then do we actively ***listen*** to the Truth in the Word of God?
Maybe we remove ourselves from political conversations that tempt us to argue in anger.
Maybe we unfollow social media accounts that tempt us to envy someone else's lifestyle.
Maybe we go to bed early to avoid the temptation of overspending online late at night.

What's one area of temptation in your life where you can commit to upholding the boundaries laid out in Proverbs 5 and actively listen for the voice of God to remain faithful?

DAY 6

PROVERBS 6

Practical Warnings & Evils God Hates

"Why can't I buy this toy?""Why does *she* get ice cream?""Why do I have to go to bed if I'm not tired?"

Kids ask a lot of questions. In today's chapter of Proverbs, Solomon continued his parental guidance by counseling his son to choose righteousness in all areas of life—and it seems he anticipated a question we've all asked our heavenly Father a time or two when He calls us to obey.

Why?

Thankfully, God gives us a better answer than "because I said so." While we can never fully understand the mind of God (Isaiah 55:9), we find motivation to dedicate our decisions to Him when we see that His decisions are motivated by deep love for us.

READ AND RESPOND

PROVERBS 6

1 My son, if you have put up se-
curity for your neighbor,
if you have shaken hands
in pledge for a stranger,
2 you have been trapped by what you said,
ensnared by the words of your mouth.
3 So do this, my son, to free yourself,
since you have fallen into
your neighbor's hands:
Go—to the point of exhaustion—
and give your neighbor no rest!
4 Allow no sleep to your eyes,
no slumber to your eyelids.
5 Free yourself, like a gazelle
from the hand of the hunter,
like a bird from the snare of the fowler.

6 Go to the ant, you sluggard;
consider its ways and be wise!
7 It has no commander,
no overseer or ruler,
8 yet it stores its provisions in summer

and gathers its food at harvest.

[9] How long will you lie
there, you sluggard?
When will you get up from your sleep?
[10] A little sleep, a little slumber,
a little folding of the hands to rest—
[11] and poverty will come
on you like a thief
and scarcity like an armed man.

[12] A troublemaker and a villain,
who goes about with a corrupt mouth,
[13] who winks maliciously with his eye,
signals with his feet
and motions with his fingers,
[14] who plots evil with de-
ceit in his heart—
he always stirs up conflict.
[15] Therefore disaster will over-
take him in an instant;
he will suddenly be de-
stroyed—without remedy.

[16] There are six things the LORD hates,
seven that are detestable to him:
[17] haughty eyes,
a lying tongue,
hands that shed innocent blood,
[18] a heart that
devises wicked schemes,
feet that are quick to rush into evil,
[19] a false witness who pours out lies
and a person who stirs up
conflict in the community.

WARNING AGAINST ADULTERY

[20] My son, keep your father's command
and do not forsake your
mother's teaching.
[21] Bind them always on your heart;
fasten them around your neck.
[22] When you walk, they will guide you;
when you sleep, they
will watch over you;
when you awake, they will speak to you.
[23] For this command is a lamp,
this teaching is a light,
and correction and instruction
are the way to life,
[24] keeping you from your neighbor's wife,
from the smooth talk of
a wayward woman.

[25] Do not lust in your heart
after her beauty
or let her captivate you with her eyes.

[26] For a prostitute can be
had for a loaf of bread,
but another man's wife
preys on your very life.

27 Can a man scoop fire into his lap
without his clothes being burned?
28 Can a man walk on hot coals
without his feet being scorched?
29 So is he who sleeps with an-
other man's wife;
no one who touches her
will go unpunished.

30 People do not despise a thief if he steals
to satisfy his hunger
when he is starving.
31 Yet if he is caught, he
must pay sevenfold,
though it costs him all the
wealth of his house.
32 But a man who commits
adultery has no sense;
whoever does so destroys himself.
33 Blows and disgrace are his lot,
and his shame will never be wiped away.

34 For jealousy arouses a husband's fury,
and he will show no
mercy when he takes revenge.
35 He will not accept any compensation;
he will refuse a bribe, how-
ever great it is.

Read and compare verses 3–11.

In what circumstances do you get yourself into trouble most often?

What is the repeated command Solomon offers his son specifically in verses 3 and 5 as it relates to his ability to affect his own circumstances?

Why do you suppose Solomon gave his son the encouragement that he has a choice in his behaviors and decisions before he gave examples of all the negative directions his decisions could lead him in?

Read Proverbs 6:16–19. Perhaps surprisingly, God's love for us is revealed even in the catalog of *"things that the LORD hates."*

In your own words, what seven things does God hate (vv. 16–19)?

1.

2.

3.

4.

5.

6.

7.

Is there anything you're surprised to see (or not see) on this list?

What does God's hatred of these things tell you about what He loves?

Try writing down the *opposite* of the seven sins in Proverbs 6:16–19; then compare your list to Galatians 5:22–23 in the chart below:

OPPOSITE OF THE SEVEN SINS IN PROVERBS 6:16-19	FRUITS OF THE SPIRIT IN GALATIANS 5:22-23	WHAT DO I NOTICE MOST?
Example: humble or modest eyes	Love Joy Peace Forbearance Kindness Goodness Faithfulness Gentleness Self-control	Example: humility results in all the fruits of the Spirit
Example: honest tongue		Example: honesty bears kindness, goodness, and love

Proverbs 6 shows that God is not indifferent to sin—because He wants to protect us from dishonesty, selfishness, and other evils that destroy our relationships with one another and with Him.

If God didn't warn us against sin, He wouldn't be a very loving Father.

Keeping this in mind, we can see that Solomon's own fatherly warnings against the *"sluggard"* (v. 9), the *"troublemaker"* (v. 12), and the *"wayward woman"* (v. 24) in today's reading may sound harsh, but they're meant to be instructional, not insulting.

God is not
indifferent to sin.

Read John 8:3–11. What did Jesus tell the woman caught in adultery to *"leave,"* and how was this an act of love?

Read 2 Thessalonians 3:10–12. What does Paul *"command and urge"* followers of Jesus to do in regard to idleness (being a *"sluggard"*) and being *"disruptive"*?

How might this apply to how you are approaching your life today?

Proverbs 6 reminds us sin is costly. The chapter begins with a warning about unwise lending (vv. 1–5), and the closing verses describe how moral debts can also accumulate and become unaffordable. The thief, for example, owes everything to the one who catches him stealing (v. 31). The person who commits adultery owes much more than *"gifts"* to the one whose marriage they violated (vv. 34–35).

And how much more must this be true of our relationship with God? Surely the human revenge described in Proverbs 6 pales in comparison to God's just vengeance over sin (1 Thessalonians 4:6).

But there's good news, friend. Proverbs 6:33–34 (ESV) justly warns that the person who does evil to another *"will get wounds and dishonor"* and will not be spared, but Romans 8:32 (ESV) declares God *"did not spare his own Son but gave him up for us all."* For all who believe in Him, Jesus has taken our wounds and paid the price for our sin forever! In Christ, we no longer relate to God as debtors but as daughters and sons.

Read Colossians 2:13–14 in contrast to Proverbs 6:33–34. What does this teach you about God's love?

In what ways might you receive the instructions or warning from Proverbs 6 and use this as wisdom in your daily decisions?

DAY 7

PROVERBS 7

Who Is Influencing You & How?

The average person in the US is exposed to as many as 10,000 advertisements daily.[1] Whether we're driving to work, ordering lunch, or Googling a question about the weird noise our dishwasher started making, we're surrounded by eye-catching billboards, promotions, and unnervingly specific pop-up ads for kitchen appliances we supposedly can't live without.

READ AND RESPOND

PROVERBS 7

1 My son, keep my words
and store up my commands within you.
2 Keep my commands and you will live;
guard my teachings as
the apple of your eye.
3 Bind them on your fingers;
write them on the tablet of your heart.
4 Say to wisdom, "You are my sister,"
and to insight, "You are my relative."
5 They will keep you from
the adulterous woman,
from the wayward woman
with her seductive words.

6 At the window of my house
I looked down through the lattice.
7 I saw among the simple,
I noticed among the young men,
a youth who had no sense.
8 He was going down the
street near her corner,
walking along in the di-
rection of her house
9 at twilight, as the day was fading,
as the dark of night set in.

10 Then out came a woman to meet him,
dressed like a prostitute
and with crafty intent.
11 (She is unruly and defiant,
her feet never stay at home;
12 now in the street, now in the squares,

at every corner she lurks.)
13 She took hold of him and kissed him
and with a brazen face she said:

14 "Today I fulfilled my vows,
and I have food from my fel-
lowship offering at home.
15 So I came out to meet you;
I looked for you and have found you!
16 I have covered my bed
with colored linens from Egypt.
17 I have perfumed my bed
with myrrh, aloes and cinnamon.
18 Come, let's drink
deeply of love till morning;
let's enjoy ourselves with love!
19 My husband is not at home;
he has gone on a long journey.
20 He took his purse filled with money
and will not be home till full moon."
21 With persuasive words
she led him astray;
she seduced him with her smooth talk.
22 All at once he followed her
like an ox going to the slaughter,
like a deer stepping into a noose
23 till an arrow pierces his liver,
like a bird darting into a snare,
little knowing it will cost him his life.

24 Now then, my sons, listen to me;
pay attention to what I say.
25 Do not let your heart turn to her ways
or stray into her paths.
26 Many are the victims she
has brought down;
her slain are a mighty throng.
27 Her house is a highway to the grave,
leading down to the chambers of death.

In many ways, the *"seductive speech"* of the adulterous woman in Proverbs 7:10–21 reads like an advertisement for sin—an enticing promise of pleasure at a small price. However, Solomon's message here is "buyer beware."

The pleasures of sin appeal to our senses and our desire for instant gratification, which explains the focus on luxurious linens, perfumes, and "enjoyment" in the woman's sales pitch (vv. 16–18).

Read the truth of falling for ungodly influence or enticement in verse 23.

Everyone who buys into sin eventually realizes *"it will cost him his life."* This applies to hidden sin, like we see in verse 9.

Read verse 9. When and in what circumstances is the meeting of these lovers described?

How often do we deceive ourselves into thinking we disobey in secret? Consider to yourself a few times you disobeyed in secret, or so you thought, and write down any consequences you experienced from the "secret sinning." Be mindful that sometimes consequences can be feelings of guilt, shame, or fear of being found out.

Look up Luke 8:17. What does Scripture say about secrets?

In his commentary on Proverbs 7, John Trapp wrote, "Foolish men think to hide themselves from God, by hiding God from themselves."[2]

What decisions might you make differently today if you truly believed nothing is kept secret from God?

Look carefully at verses 6–14. Aside from meeting under cover of darkness, we also see the woman use hypocrisy to justify her sin: *"I had food for my fellowship offering,"* she explains, likely referring to offerings in a pagan temple.

Make a brief list of how this woman is described, including her motives and actions. What do you notice about her?

Read verses 14–21 again. Her speech is not only sensually seductive but theologically seductive. She tempts with a false religion that says, "As long as you go through the motions at church, it's OK to live however you want, bouncing back and forth between worship and wickedness."

Today we don't make temple sacrifices, but have you ever hoped God would overlook disobedience in one area of your life because of your obedience in another area? What's the problem with this logic? (See Romans 6:1–2 and Matthew 23:25.)

What does 1 Samuel 15:22 say is *"better than sacrifice"*?

It seems the woman in Proverbs 7 sees God as one more "customer" to negotiate with through sacrifices and vows to compensate for her sin. But that's not who God is. He faithfully loves us and wants what's best for us, so He doesn't take bribes or accept the false currency of halfhearted "good deeds." In fact, God is not interested in a *transaction*—He invites us into a *relationship* with Him.

God is not interested in a *transaction*—
He invites us into a *relationship* with Him.

Unlike earthly pleasures that last only *"till morning"* (Proverbs 7:18), God offers us everlasting life in Christ. His love is not a commodity; it's a covenant. So let's make choices based on His trustworthy promises instead of the world's persuasions and remember where real treasure is found.

To wrap up today's study, let's read the advice of the Lord through the prophet Isaiah as we consider who we allow to influence us and who we are listening to:

Give ear and come to me;
listen, that you may live.
I will make an everlasting covenant with you,
my faithful love promised to David. (Isaiah 55:3)

DAY 8

PROVERBS 8

The Beauty of Wisdom Is Praised

Reading Proverbs can feel very different from reading other scriptural genres like history, narrative, or poetry. There's no plot to follow, and sometimes we might struggle to see any obvious connections between Proverbs and the gospel of Jesus. Is the whole Bible really cross-shaped?

Spoiler alert: Yes! Today we'll see clearly how the wisdom of King Solomon points us to the greater wisdom of King Jesus.

Remember how we read about Lady Wisdom on Day 1 of our study? We hear from her again in today's Scriptures; however, the *ESV Study Bible* notes that Proverbs 8 "seems to go beyond personification to describing a personality, which has led to discussions of whether Christians should relate this description to Christ."[1]

READ AND RESPOND

PROVERBS 8

1 Does not wisdom call out?
Does not understanding raise her voice?
2 At the highest point along the way,
where the paths meet,
she takes her stand;
3 beside the gate leading into the city,
at the entrance, she cries aloud:
4 "To you, O people, I call out;
I raise my voice to all mankind.
5 You who are simple, gain prudence;
you who are foolish, set your hearts on it.
6 Listen, for I have trustworthy things to say;
I open my lips to speak what is right.
7 My mouth speaks what is true,
for my lips detest wickedness.
8 All the words of my mouth are just;
none of them is crooked or perverse.
9 To the discerning all of them are right;
they are upright to those who have found knowledge.
10 Choose my instruction instead of silver,

knowledge rather than choice gold,
11 for wisdom is more pre-
cious than rubies,
and nothing you desire
can compare with her.

12 "I, wisdom, dwell
together with prudence;
I possess knowledge and discretion.
13 To fear the LORD is to hate evil;
I hate pride and arrogance,
evil behavior and perverse speech.
14 Counsel and sound judgment are mine;
I have insight, I have power.
15 By me kings reign
and rulers issue decrees that are just;
16 by me princes govern,
and nobles—all who rule on earth.
17 I love those who love me,
and those who seek me find me.
18 With me are riches and honor,
enduring wealth and prosperity.
19 My fruit is better than fine gold;
what I yield surpasses choice silver.
20 I walk in the way of righteousness,
along the paths of justice,
21 bestowing a rich inheri-
tance on those who love me
and making their treasuries full.

22 "The LORD brought me forth
as the first of his works,
before his deeds of old;
23 I was formed long ages ago,
at the very beginning, when
the world came to be.
24 When there were no watery
depths, I was given birth,
when there were no springs
overflowing with water;
25 before the mountains
were settled in place,
before the hills, I was given birth,
26 before he made the world or its fields
or any of the dust of the earth.
27 I was there when he set
the heavens in place,
when he marked out the hori-
zon on the face of the deep,
28 when he established the clouds above
and fixed securely the foun-
tains of the deep,
29 when he gave the sea its boundary
so the waters would not
overstep his command,
and when he marked out the
foundations of the earth.
30 Then I was constantly at his side.
I was filled with delight day after day,
rejoicing always in his presence,
31 rejoicing in his whole world
and delighting in mankind.

32 "Now then, my children, listen to me;
blessed are those who keep my ways.
33 Listen to my instruction and be wise;
do not disregard it.
34 Blessed are those who listen to me,
watching daily at my doors,
waiting at my doorway.
35 For those who find me find life
and receive favor from the LORD.
36 But those who fail to find
me harm themselves;
all who hate me love death."

Let's look at a few key verses that scholars highlight as pointing to Jesus:

WISDOM	JESUS
In Proverbs 8:7-8, Wisdom says, *"My mouth speaks what is ___________ . . . . All the words of my mouth are __________."*	What did the apostle Peter say about Jesus' words in John 6:68-69?
In Proverbs 8:21, Wisdom claims to grant *"a ________________ on those who love me."*	According to 1 Peter 1:3-5, how do we receive this from God?
In Proverbs 8:22-31, Wisdom describes God's creation of the world and says in verse 30, *"I was ___________ at his _________."*	According to John 1:1-4, where was Jesus and what was He doing when the world was created?

> There is only one Savior who speaks words of eternal life, secures a heavenly inheritance for those who love Him, and was present with God at the beginning of time! That Savior is Jesus.

But wait a minute. How can the **Son** of God be **Lady** Wisdom? This is an important question, and David Guzik helps us understand it this way:

> Because Jesus *is* God, He has and expresses and demonstrates the wisdom of God; but the *woman* of Proverbs 8 does not directly describe Jesus.[2]

In other words, Lady Wisdom is a symbolic figure who draws our attention and our affections to our very real Savior. It's sort of like how the shadow of a bird might make us look for the real animal in the sky—but we know the shadow is not the bird. As a shadow of Christ, Lady Wisdom says she *"was formed"* and *"given birth"* by God (vv. 23–24)—but **Jesus is God**. He has always eternally existed.

Because Jesus is eternal, how long will His *"enduring wealth and prosperity"* endure (v. 18)?

Because Jesus did the mountain-shaping, limit-assigning, foundation-laying work described in Proverbs 8:22–31, what knowledge does He have that no one else has?

Although Proverbs was written about 1,000 years before Jesus came to earth to redeem us through His life, death, and resurrection, God was already weaving His Son's wisdom and love into His Word. The plan was already in progress. God had already made His choice. Now He calls us to make ours: *"Listen to me; blessed are those who keep my ways . . . For those who find me find life"* (Proverbs 8:32–35).

How does seeing Jesus at the center of Proverbs shape your reading and response to *"listen to me"* (v. 32)?

In what specific ways will you use words of Proverbs 8 to make wise decisions today?

DAY 9

PROVERBS 9

Choosing Wisdom or Folly

In a movie scene where a character weighs pros and cons of a big decision, sometimes a tiny, white-winged angel and a tiny, red-tailed devil appear on her shoulders, each whispering competing advice. The devil rants and waves his pitchfork while the angel, halo shimmering, calmly explains how to take the "high road."

In today's reading, we see a similar battle of wills between wisdom and folly, each calling people to feast with them. The two feasts take place in very different locations—heaven and hell (also called "Sheol" in the Old Testament). But interestingly, both wisdom and folly initially extend the same invitation: *"Let all who are simple come to my house!"* (vv. 4, 16).

READ AND RESPOND

PROVERBS 9

1 Wisdom has built her house;
she has set up its seven pillars.
2 She has prepared her meat
and mixed her wine;
she has also set her table.
3 She has sent out her ser-
vants, and she calls
from the highest point of the city,
4 "Let all who are sim-
ple come to my house!"
To those who have no sense she says,
5 "Come, eat my food
and drink the wine I have mixed.
6 Leave your simple ways
and you will live;
walk in the way of insight."

7 Whoever corrects a
mocker invites insults;
whoever rebukes the
wicked incurs abuse.
8 Do not rebuke mock-
ers or they will hate you;
rebuke the wise and they will love you.

9 Instruct the wise and they
will be wiser still;
teach the righteous and they
will add to their learning.

10 The fear of the LORD is the
beginning of wisdom,
and knowledge of the Holy
One is understanding.
11 For through wisdom your
days will be many,
and years will be added to your life.
12 If you are wise, your wis-
dom will reward you;
if you are a mocker, you
alone will suffer.

13 Folly is an unruly woman;
she is simple and knows nothing.
14 She sits at the door of her house,
on a seat at the highest point of the city,
15 calling out to those who pass by,
who go straight on their way,
16 "Let all who are sim-
ple come to my house!"
To those who have no sense she says,
17 "Stolen water is sweet;
food eaten in secret is delicious!"
18 But little do they know
that the dead are there,
that her guests are deep in
the realm of the dead.

Read Proverbs 9:4. Who speaks these words first: wisdom or folly? Why might this be important?

Scholars suggest that in verse 16, we hear folly impersonating wisdom's call for evil purposes. This interpretation of Proverbs 9 tells a tale as old as time: In the beginning, God, the Creator, told Adam and Eve, *"You are free to eat from any tree in the garden; but you must not eat from the tree of the knowledge of good and evil . . . you will certainly die"* (Genesis 2:16–17). Satan, the imitator, repeated God's words but with a deceitful twist: *"Did God really say, 'You must not eat from any tree in the garden'? . . . You will not certainly die"* (Genesis 3:1–4).

Read Matthew 4:5–7. Similarly, how did Satan tempt Jesus?

How did Jesus respond?

For thousands of years, the enemy has been concealing ugly lies in packaging that resembles truth. But we don't have to fall for his tricks. The more intimately we know God and His Word, the more we can detect and reject Satan's deceptions.

For example, Proverbs 9:17 says, *"Stolen water is sweet; food eaten in secret is delicious!"* Using the following chart, how do the truths about Jesus in John 6:35 and John 4:10–14 combat these false claims?

FOLLY'S LIE:

"Stolen water is sweet; food eaten in secret is delicious!"

Proverbs 9:16

	List the truths about Jesus that combat folly's lie
Then Jesus declared, "I am the bread of life. Whoever comes to me will never go hungry, and whoever believes in me will never be thirsty." John 6:35	

10 Jesus answered her, "If you knew the gift of God and who it is that asks you for a drink, you would have asked him and he would have given you living water."

11 "Sir," the woman said, "you have nothing to draw with and the well is deep. Where can you get this living water? 12 Are you greater than our father Jacob, who gave us the well and drank from it himself, as did also his sons and his livestock?"

13 Jesus answered, "Everyone who drinks this water will be thirsty again, 14 but whoever drinks the water I give them will never thirst. Indeed, the water I give them will become in them a spring of water welling up to eternal life."

John 4:10–14

We might wonder why wisdom even bothers calling out to *"simple"* people in today's reading (v. 4). Why do you think so much effort is spent speaking to and about the simple in this Proverb?

As we ask this question, there's one key truth to remember: We're the simple ones. The Hebrew word translated *simple* in both Proverbs 9:4 and Proverbs 9:16 describes someone naive and susceptible to influence[1]—which is to say, every sinner under the sun. We all know so little and need so much from God. When He grows wisdom and righteousness in us, He always starts from scratch.

How does Proverbs 9:10 confirm that becoming wise starts with admitting we need God?

Growing in wisdom requires bowing in humility. However, this doesn't mean it's a completely passive process on our part. Read Proverbs 9:12 in the New Living Translation: *"If **you** become wise, **you** will be the one to benefit. If **you** scorn wisdom, **you** will be the one to suffer"* (emphases added).

Scholar Derek Kidner boldly suggested that Proverbs 9:12 is "perhaps the strongest expression of individualism in the Bible."[2] It emphasizes that although we are simple and prone to wander—and although the devil on our shoulder (so to speak) may whisper countless lies—it is our choice to listen or not. By God's grace, we can decide to listen to His wisdom and *"live"* (v. 6)!

What does this tell us about our responsibility for actively pursuing wisdom?

How can you prioritize this pursuit in your life this week?

DAY 10

PROVERBS 10

The Power of the Words We Choose

As we open up Proverbs 10, we've made it through the discourses of chapters 1–9, and now we start to see what are more immediately recognizable as *proverbs*—short, memorable sayings about vice, virtue, and values in God's Kingdom.

Each of these proverbs can be read as a standalone truth, but when we study them all together, we notice some recurring themes about the kinds of decisions that characterize a follower of God.

Bible scholars classify many of the proverbs we'll look at today as "antithetical," meaning they set up a contrast (antithesis) between the wise path of the godly and the foolish path of the wicked. The first line of an antithetical proverb often describes the ideal, and then comes an all-important *"but . . ."* followed by the opposite of the ideal.

READ AND RESPOND

PROVERBS 10

1 The proverbs of Solomon:

A wise son brings joy to his father,
but a foolish son brings
grief to his mother.

2 Ill-gotten treasures have no lasting value,
but righteousness delivers from death.

3 The LORD does not let the
righteous go hungry,
but he thwarts the
craving of the wicked.

4 Lazy hands make for poverty,
but diligent hands bring wealth.

5 He who gathers crops in sum-
mer is a prudent son,
but he who sleeps during har-
vest is a disgraceful son.

6 Blessings crown the head
of the righteous,

but violence overwhelms
the mouth of the wicked.

7 The name of the righ-
teous is used in blessings,
but the name of the wicked will rot.

8 The wise in heart accept commands,
but a chattering fool comes to ruin.

9 Whoever walks in integ-
rity walks securely,
but whoever takes
crooked paths will be found out.

10 Whoever winks mali-
ciously causes grief,
and a chattering fool comes to ruin.

11 The mouth of the righ-
teous is a fountain of life,
but the mouth of the
wicked conceals violence.

12 Hatred stirs up conflict,
but love covers over all wrongs.

13 Wisdom is found on the
lips of the discerning,
but a rod is for the back of
one who has no sense.

14 The wise store up knowledge,
but the mouth of a fool invites ruin.

15 The wealth of the rich is
their fortified city,
but poverty is the ruin of the poor.

16 The wages of the righteous is life,
but the earnings of the
wicked are sin and death.

17 Whoever heeds discipline
shows the way to life,
but whoever ignores correc-
tion leads others astray.

18 Whoever conceals ha-
tred with lying lips
and spreads slander is a fool.

19 Sin is not ended by multiplying words,
but the prudent hold their tongues.

20 The tongue of the righ-
teous is choice silver,
but the heart of the
wicked is of little value.

21 The lips of the righteous nourish many,
but fools die for lack of sense.

22 The blessing of the
LORD brings wealth,
without painful toil for it.

23 A fool finds pleasure in
wicked schemes,
but a person of understand-
ing delights in wisdom.

24 What the wicked dread
will overtake them;
what the righteous de-
sire will be granted.

25 When the storm has swept
by, the wicked are gone,
but the righteous stand firm forever.

26 As vinegar to the teeth
and smoke to the eyes,
so are sluggards to those
who send them.

27 The fear of the LORD
adds length to life,
but the years of the
wicked are cut short.

28 The prospect of the righteous is joy,
but the hopes of the
wicked come to nothing.

29 The way of the LORD is a ref-
uge for the blameless,
but it is the ruin of those who do evil.

30 The righteous will never be uprooted,
but the wicked will not re-
main in the land.

31 From the mouth of the righ-
teous comes the fruit of wisdom,
but a perverse tongue will be silenced.

32 The lips of the righteous
know what finds favor,
but the mouth of the
wicked only what is perverse.

Chart the following verses here:

VERSE	THE RIGHTEOUS PERSON (IDEAL)		THE WICKED PERSON (OPPOSITE)
11	The mouth is a fountain of life.		The mouth conceals violence.
14			
20		B	
21		U	
31		T	
32			

What repeated ideas about lips, mouths, and words do you notice in Proverbs 10?

One commentary puts it this way: **"Speak well, get blessed; speak badly, get blasted."**[1] Simple enough! But of course, this is much easier said than done. And the stakes are higher than we might think: Not only do our word choices result in either "blessing" or "blasting" for us personally, but they also profoundly affect the people around us.

Foolish or evil words are linked with violence, ruin, and even death throughout Proverbs 10. But verse 11 says thoughtful, righteous words are a *"fountain of life"*—and when we read the proverb in its Ancient Near Eastern context, we can see this as an image of *communal blessing*. In the deserts of Israel, fountains, wells, or springs served as public gathering spaces where community members and passing travelers alike often met to refresh themselves, draw water for their homes, and share conversation. Villages were often built near a water source, which would naturally become a hub of hospitality.[2]

List some examples of life-giving and refreshing words that invite others to gather together in community. These could be words you've said or ones spoken by others.

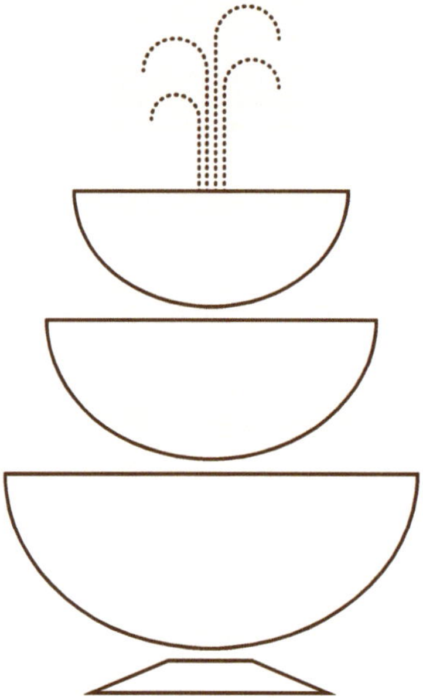

Now list some words you've said or heard recently that were more like a drain than a fountain (untrue, careless, discouraging, unkind, etc.). If you spoke these words, confess them to the Lord, and receive His forgiveness. He gives more grace (James 4:6)!

As we continue studying **antithetical proverbs,** we'll likely find ourselves on the wrong side of the *"but . . ."* more often than we'd like to admit. None of us makes the right decision or says the right thing 100 percent of the time. But does this mean we're among *"the wicked"* whose hearts Proverbs 10:20 says are *"of little value"* ?

Well, we know we were wicked once—because everyone is wicked before turning to Christ in faith. He is the only perfectly righteous One. But we also know what 1 Peter 3:18 says: *"For Christ also suffered once for sins, the righteous for the unrighteous, to bring you to God"*

Therefore, the Scriptures in Proverbs are for our encouragement and warning, both the ones about the righteous and the ones about the wicked.

Jesus used His words to *"nourish many"* (Proverbs 10:21) during His life on earth, and His words continue to feed us today.

In what ways do you see your words having power over your daily circumstances?

How might spending time in Scripture shape your words to nourish those who receive them like Jesus' words did?

DAY 11

PROVERBS 11

The Path of the Righteous Leads to God

Have you ever heard the saying "What goes around comes around"? It's a reminder that actions have consequences, specifically implying that what we do determines what will later be done to us. But when we're tempted to disobey God, we often disregard the consequences.

It's a harmless indulgence. Nobody will get hurt.
Other people do it all the time, and they seem fine.
This won't hinder me—it will help me.

Do these thoughts sound familiar to you? What kinds of excuses or justifications cross your mind when you're tempted to make an unwise choice?

We often try to justify wrong choices when they look like shortcuts to success, acceptance, ease, or happiness. If we just cut this one little corner, we can get promoted faster . . . make more friends . . . avoid that uncomfortable conversation . . . keep that dark secret. But Proverbs 11 confirms that this path is actually a circle, not a shortcut.

READ AND RESPOND

PROVERBS 11

1 The Lord detests dishonest scales,
but accurate weights
find favor with him.

2 When pride comes, then comes disgrace,
but with humility comes wisdom.

3 The integrity of the up-
right guides them,
but the unfaithful are de-
stroyed by their duplicity.

4 Wealth is worthless in the day of wrath,
but righteousness delivers from death.

5 The righteousness of the blame-
less makes their paths straight,
but the wicked are brought

down by their own wickedness.

6 The righteousness of the up-
right delivers them,
but the unfaithful are
trapped by evil desires.

7 Hopes placed in mortals die with them;
all the promise of their
power comes to nothing.

8 The righteous person is res-
cued from trouble,
and it falls on the wicked instead.

9 With their mouths the god-
less destroy their neighbors,
but through knowledge
the righteous escape.

10 When the righteous pros-
per, the city rejoices;
when the wicked perish,
there are shouts of joy.

11 Through the blessing of the
upright a city is exalted,
but by the mouth of the
wicked it is destroyed.

12 Whoever derides their
neighbor has no sense,
but the one who has under-
standing holds their tongue.

13 A gossip betrays a confidence,
but a trustworthy person keeps a secret.

14 For lack of guidance a nation falls,
but victory is won through
many advisers.

15 Whoever puts up security for
a stranger will surely suffer,
but whoever refuses to shake
hands in pledge is safe.

16 A kindhearted woman gains honor,
but ruthless men gain only wealth.

17 Those who are kind benefit themselves,
but the cruel bring ruin on themselves.

18 A wicked person earns deceptive wages,
but the one who sows righ-
teousness reaps a sure reward.

19 Truly the righteous attain life,
but whoever pursues evil finds death.

20 The LORD detests those
whose hearts are perverse,

but he delights in those
whose ways are blameless.

21 Be sure of this: The
wicked will not go unpunished,
but those who are righ-
teous will go free.

22 Like a gold ring in a pig's snout
is a beautiful woman who
shows no discretion.

23 The desire of the righ-
teous ends only in good,
but the hope of the
wicked only in wrath.

24 One person gives
freely, yet gains even more;
another withholds
unduly, but comes to poverty.

25 A generous person will prosper;
whoever refreshes oth-
ers will be refreshed.

26 People curse the one who hoards grain,
but they pray God's blessing on
the one who is willing to sell.

27 Whoever seeks good finds favor,
but evil comes to one
who searches for it.

28 Those who trust in their riches will fall,
but the righteous will
thrive like a green leaf.

29 Whoever brings ruin on their
family will inherit only wind,
and the fool will be servant to the wise.

30 The fruit of the righ-
teous is a tree of life,
and the one who is wise saves lives.

31 If the righteous receive
their due on earth,
how much more the un-
godly and the sinner!

As we read in these verses, sin doubles back on itself such that *"the wicked are brought down by **their own** wickedness . . . the unfaithful are trapped by **[their]** evil desires"* (vv. 5–6), and *"the cruel bring ruin on **themselves**"* (v. 17, emphases added).

What goes around comes around.

Have you ever made a wrong decision you thought would never catch up with you, but it did? What did you learn about yourself and about God from this experience?

How does your experience compare to Proverbs 11:3 and to Adam and Eve's experience in the garden of Eden in Genesis 3?

Thankfully, Proverbs 11 reminds us that the path of righteousness is circular too—but in the best way. When we choose to follow God, He leads us on a journey back to a perfect heavenly paradise much like the garden of Eden He created in the beginning. Scripture tells us heaven will be a lot like Eden was before sin entered the world—complete with a life-giving river (Revelation 22:1; Genesis 2:10), fruitful trees (Revelation 22:2; Genesis 1:12) and glorious light (Revelation 21:23; Genesis 1:3).

Read Proverbs 11 slowly and fill in the chart, noting characteristics, examples, and results of both righteousness and wickedness:

RIGHTEOUSNESS	WICKEDNESS
Example:	
v. 1 accurate calculating finds favor	v. 1 dishonest calculating is detested
v. 2 humility/wisdom	v. 2 pride/disgrace

Read Proverbs 11:30. Fill in the blanks:

"The fruit of the righteous is ______________________________,

and the one who is wise ______________________________."

Interestingly, the words *tree of life* show up in only three books in the Bible: Genesis, Proverbs, and Revelation.

In Genesis (a book the original readers of Proverbs would have known well), God banished rebellious humans from Eden so they couldn't eat from the *"tree of life"* (Genesis 3:23–24).

In Revelation, God has promised to eternally reverse this banishment for believers in Jesus: He will *"give the right to eat from the tree of life"* in heaven with Him forever (Revelation 2:7).

And Proverbs? One could say it tells us what to do in the middle. As we live out our days between Genesis and Revelation, we can choose to walk God's righteous path—knowing that it leads from garden to garden, and from life to everlasting life (Proverbs 11:4; Proverbs 11:19).

> How does it change the way you make choices when you think about where the path of righteousness leads: to paradise with God or to the path of sin?

Every decision leads to a destination.

DAY 12

PROVERBS 12

Righteousness Is Not Blessing-Seeking

At this point in our study, you may be noticing a theme in Proverbs that goes something like this: God rewards the righteous. As for the wicked? Not so much.

For many of us, the book of Proverbs may raise some questions—namely, does God have a different definition of things like "harm" or "trouble" than we do? It seems like we don't have to look far in our world to find examples of bad things happening to righteous people. Let's see how Proverbs 12 guides us to a deeper understanding of what righteous living looks like.

READ AND RESPOND

PROVERBS 12

1 Whoever loves disci-
pline loves knowledge,
but whoever hates correction is stupid.

2 Good people obtain fa-
vor from the LORD,
but he condemns those who
devise wicked schemes.

3 No one can be established
through wickedness,
but the righteous cannot be uprooted.

4 A wife of noble character
is her husband's crown,
but a disgraceful wife is
like decay in his bones.

5 The plans of the righteous are just,
but the advice of the
wicked is deceitful.

6 The words of the
wicked lie in wait for blood,
but the speech of the
upright rescues them.

7 The wicked are over-
thrown and are no more,
but the house of the righ-

teous stands firm.

8 A person is praised according
to their prudence,
and one with a warped
mind is despised.

9 Better to be a nobody and
yet have a servant
than pretend to be somebody
and have no food.

10 The righteous care for the
needs of their animals,
but the kindest acts of
the wicked are cruel.

11 Those who work their land
will have abundant food,
but those who chase fantasies
have no sense.

12 The wicked desire the stronghold
of evildoers,
but the root of the righteous endures.

13 Evildoers are trapped
by their sinful talk,
and so the innocent escape trouble.

14 From the fruit of their lips people
are filled with good things,
and the work of their hands
brings them reward.

15 The way of fools seems right to them,
but the wise listen to advice.

16 Fools show their annoyance at once,
but the prudent overlook an insult.

17 An honest witness tells the truth,
but a false witness tells lies.

18 The words of the reckless
pierce like swords,
but the tongue of the
wise brings healing.

19 Truthful lips endure forever,
but a lying tongue lasts only a moment.

20 Deceit is in the hearts of
those who plot evil,
but those who promote peace have joy.

21 No harm overtakes the righteous,
but the wicked have their fill of trouble.

22 The LORD detests lying lips,
but he delights in people
who are trustworthy.

23 The prudent keep their
knowledge to themselves,
but a fool's heart blurts out folly.

24 Diligent hands will rule,
but laziness ends in forced labor.

25 Anxiety weighs down the heart,
but a kind word cheers it up.

26 The righteous choose
their friends carefully,
but the way of the
wicked leads them astray.

27 The lazy do not roast any game,
but the diligent feed on
the riches of the hunt.

28 In the way of righteousness there is life;
along that path is immortality.

A glance into the intensive care unit, the marriage counselor's office, or sometimes even the mirror reveals pain that seems to contradict the claim we find today in verse 21: *"No harm overtakes the righteous, but the wicked have their fill of trouble."*

Remember when we discussed on page 7 of this guide how proverbs are not the same as *guarantees* from God? How might that distinction help you understand this verse?

It's also important to remember that only Christ Himself is perfectly righteous. From that perspective, it actually makes sense that our lives are troubled. We are all fallen people who live in a fallen world. However, we know that believers are counted righteous by placing our trust in Jesus.

Read Psalm 56:11 and Psalm 118:6.

What question is repeated by people who trusted in God?

In one sense, we know humans can do many terrible things. But the heart of this question isn't actually about what harm may or may not come to God's people—it's about how *"the LORD is with me"* **no matter what comes** (Psalm 118:6). With this in mind, we can conclude that Proverbs 12:21 likewise does not guarantee a trouble-free life but a blessed life, in which God will "manage the degree of trouble, the duration of trouble, and the depth of the trouble" for those who love Him.[1]

Does this truth feel discouraging or encouraging—or both—to you in your circumstances today? Why?

Proverbs 12:7 echoes the assurance that God rewards and strengthens His people: *"The house of the righteous stands firm."* Yet it's also true that standing on the Lord can be hard. In fact, the Hebrew word *amad* ("stand") also means "endure, persist or survive,"[2] which implies difficulty—and reminds us to check our motives for pursuing righteousness in the first place.

Read each verse of Proverbs 12 and make a comparison list in the chart below to more clearly see how God outlines for us what comes from following His way and what comes from turning from it.

GOD'S WAY, GOD'S BLESSING	NOT GOD'S WAY, CERTAIN CONSEQUENCES
Example: v. 1 discipline, knowledge v. 2 goodness, favor	v. 1 hates correction, stupidity v. 2 wicked schemes, condemned

Do we seek to live righteously because it pleases God . . . or because God's blessings please us?

It's important to consider and be honest about our motivations in every decision we make. When we tell the truth instead of a convenient lie, are we content that our honesty brings God *"delight"* (v. 22)? Or do we secretly hope for a better blessing? Ask yourself the following tough questions and respond honestly, knowing God gives us alternatives to every temptation and every sin:

> No temptation has overtaken you except what is common to mankind. And God is faithful; he will not let you be tempted beyond what you can bear. But when you are tempted, he will also provide a way out so that you can endure it.
>
> 1 CORINTHIANS 10:13

When a friend speaks hurtful words, in what ways do you find it natural or difficult to respond with grace (v. 16)?

Have you ever felt resentful that God allows us to be insulted or humiliated? What has been the result? In what ways did your resentment affect your decisions moving on from the circumstance?

In what ways is it challenging for you to humbly accept and truly believe that *"good people obtain favor from the LORD"* (v. 2)?

Or do you more often find yourself considering goodness like a bargaining chip: *I did the right thing, so God owes me a favor*?

The wonderful truth is that when we seek more and more of God because we love Him, we receive His good gifts too! But when we seek more and more gifts because we love blessings, we risk missing out on the Giver.

> Let's take an honest inventory of our own hearts. How or when have you seen blessing-seeking behavior creep into your walk with God?

> What new choices could you make, or what good choices could you reinforce, to ensure that pursuing God Himself is your first priority?

DAY 13

PROVERBS 13

Godly Instruction Given in Love Is a Blessing

The US National Highway Traffic Safety Administration once debuted a public safety campaign with a now-iconic slogan: "Friends don't let friends drink and drive." We can probably think of other things "friends don't let friends" do, because the principle remains true: If we care about someone, we'll advise them against making dangerous choices.

In today's Bible reading, we see a similar idea. While reiterating several themes we've already mentioned this week, including righteous speech and God's blessings for the righteous, Proverbs 13 emphasizes that righteous people both **need** and **accept** godly instruction—even when that instruction takes the form of *"correction"* (v. 18) or *"rebuke"* (v. 1).

READ AND RESPOND

PROVERBS 13

1 A wise son heeds his father's instruction,
but a mocker does not
respond to rebukes.

2 From the fruit of their lips
people enjoy good things,
but the unfaithful have an
appetite for violence.

3 Those who guard their lips
preserve their lives,
but those who speak rashly
will come to ruin.

4 A sluggard's appetite is never filled,
but the desires of the
diligent are fully satisfied.

5 The righteous hate what is false,
but the wicked make
themselves a stench
and bring shame on themselves.

6 Righteousness guards the
person of integrity,
but wickedness overthrows the sinner.

7 One person pretends to be
rich, yet has nothing;
another pretends to be poor,
yet has great wealth.

8 A person's riches may ransom their life,
but the poor cannot respond
to threatening rebukes.

9 The light of the righteous
shines brightly,
but the lamp of the
wicked is snuffed out.

10 Where there is strife, there is pride,
but wisdom is found in
those who take advice.

11 Dishonest money dwindles away,
but whoever gathers money
little by little makes it grow.

12 Hope deferred makes the heart sick,
but a longing fulfilled is a tree of life.

13 Whoever scorns instruction
will pay for it,
but whoever respects a
command is rewarded.

14 The teaching of the wise
is a fountain of life,
turning a person from
the snares of death.

15 Good judgment wins favor,
but the way of the unfaithful
leads to their destruction.

16 All who are prudent act
with knowledge,
but fools expose their folly.

17 A wicked messenger falls into trouble,
but a trustworthy envoy brings healing.

18 Whoever disregards discipline
comes to poverty and shame,
but whoever heeds
correction is honored.

19 A longing fulfilled is sweet to the soul,
but fools detest turning from evil.

20 Walk with the wise and become wise,
for a companion of fools suffers harm.

21 Trouble pursues the sinner,
but the righteous are rewarded
with good things.

22 A good person leaves an inheritance

for their children's children,
but a sinner's wealth is stored
up for the righteous.

23 An unplowed field produces
food for the poor,
but injustice sweeps it away.

24 Whoever spares the rod
hates their children,
but the one who loves their children
is careful to discipline them.

25 The righteous eat to
their hearts' content,
but the stomach of the
wicked goes hungry.

Do you associate correction and rebuke with righteousness? What images or ideas come to mind when you hear these words?

The claim in Proverbs 13:18—*"whoever heeds correction is honored"*—echoes what we read yesterday in Proverbs 12:1: *"Whoever loves discipline loves knowledge, but whoever hates correction is stupid."* Some translations use the word *reproof.* (Side note: King Solomon sure was a straight talker, huh?) But these bold statements might sound backward to us at first. Haven't we read Scriptures about *unrighteous* people being disciplined? Shouldn't the righteous always be gracious and wise so we never need reprimanding?

Ideally, yes! But none of us is perfect on this side of heaven, which means we can all benefit from wise advice and sometimes from loving yet firm redirection when we're heading down a wrong path.

Below are a few examples of righteous rebuke in Scripture. Who responded wisely to correction, and who didn't?

1 Samuel 2:22–25:

2 Samuel 12:1–13:

Luke 9:51–56:

God helps and encourages His people to teach, advise, and sometimes correct one another based on His Truth. Not all advice that comes our way is godly, but Proverbs 13 reveals several kinds of instruction to pay attention to.

Look at these verses and fill in the description of who we can get instruction from and/or the benefit of following instruction:

13:1 example: Instruction from one's father

13:13 ____

13:20 ____

13:24 ____

Who are some people you trust to offer godly advice? When was the last time you asked for their wisdom about a decision you were facing? (If you can't think of anyone, write a prayer asking God to bring trustworthy advisers into your life.)

Is there anyone whose advice you should *stop* following?

Based on Proverbs 13, what kinds of counsel or reproof should God's people *not* listen to?

The *ESV Study Bible* remarks that "hardness in unteachability" is "the great sin in Proverbs."[1] Godly counsel—even correction—keeps our hearts soft and ready to learn. With this in mind, here are a few ways we can seek *"the teaching of the wise"* (v. 14):

1. PRAY FOR COUNSEL AND CORRECTION.

It might sound something like this: *God, I know I'm not perfect, and I need help to follow You faithfully. Please use Your Word, Your Spirit, and Your people to teach me Your ways so I can keep learning and changing.*

2. BE THANKFUL FOR COUNSEL AND CORRECTION.

Instead of being surprised or offended, we can accept necessary reproof as a part of life. Roses are red. Violets are blue. Sometimes we all need a good talking-to. In fact, we can thank God for His kindness to lovingly turn us away *"from the snares of death"* (Proverbs 13:14)!

3. ASK FOR COUNSEL AND CORRECTION.

By inviting trusted, God-fearing friends to speak into our decision-making, we can live out the truth of Proverbs 13:20: *"Walk with the wise and become wise, for a companion of fools suffers harm."*

Which of these practices could you start incorporating into your life this week? (P.S. You don't have to pick just one!)

In what specific ways might one or more of the verses in Proverbs 13 positively influence how you make daily decisions? Write the verse and claim the positive impact here:

DAY 14

PROVERBS 14

Discernment in Decisions

What's the difference between a hippo and a Zippo?
One is really heavy, and the other is a little lighter.

Get it? Hopefully this punch line made you chuckle, but all jokes aside, the question "What's the difference?" is at the heart of today's Bible reading. We'll study several proverbs focused on discernment: knowing the difference between what's wise and what isn't.

Especially when we encounter lies disguised as truth or "gray areas" where multiple choices seem valid, we need *"the wisdom of the prudent [to] give thought to [our] ways"* (Proverbs 14:8).

DISCERNMENT

MERRIAM-WEBSTER DICTIONARY	"the quality of being able to grasp or comprehend what is obscure; skill in discerning; an act of perceiving something"
THEOLOGIAN SINCLAIR FERGUSON	"not only distinguishing the right from the wrong" but also "the primary from the secondary, the essential from the indifferent, and the permanent from the transient."[1]

What does **1 Corinthians 10:23** say about the difference between what is *"beneficial"* and what is *"constructive"*? How does this relate to discernment?

In what situations or relationships do you sense the greatest need for discernment in your life?

READ AND RESPOND

PROVERBS 14

1 The wise woman builds her house,
but with her own hands the
foolish one tears hers down.

2 Whoever fears the LORD
walks uprightly,
but those who despise him
are devious in their ways.

3 A fool's mouth lashes out with pride,
but the lips of the wise protect them.

4 Where there are no oxen,
the manger is empty,
but from the strength of an
ox come abundant harvests.

5 An honest witness does not deceive,
but a false witness pours out lies.

6 The mocker seeks wis-
dom and finds none,
but knowledge comes eas-
ily to the discerning.

7 Stay away from a fool,
for you will not find knowl-
edge on their lips.

8 The wisdom of the prudent is
to give thought to their ways,
but the folly of fools is deception.

9 Fools mock at making amends for sin,
but goodwill is found
among the upright.

10 Each heart knows its own bitterness,
and no one else can share its joy.

11 The house of the
wicked will be destroyed,
but the tent of the upright will flourish.

12 There is a way that appears to be right,
but in the end it leads to death.

13 Even in laughter the heart may ache,
and rejoicing may end in grief.

14 The faithless will be
fully repaid for their ways,
and the good rewarded for theirs.

15 The simple believe anything,
but the prudent give
thought to their steps.

16 The wise fear the LORD and shun evil,
but a fool is
hotheaded and yet feels secure.

17 A quick-tempered per-
son does foolish things,
and the one who
devises evil schemes is hated.

18 The simple inherit folly,
but the prudent are crowned
with knowledge.

19 Evildoers will bow down in
the presence of the good,
and the wicked at the
gates of the righteous.

20 The poor are shunned even
by their neighbors,
but the rich have many friends.

21 It is a sin to despise one's neighbor,
but blessed is the one who
is kind to the needy.

22 Do not those who plot evil go astray?
But those who plan what is good
find love and faithfulness.

23 All hard work brings a profit,
but mere talk leads only to poverty.

24 The wealth of the wise is their crown,
but the folly of fools yields folly.

25 A truthful witness saves lives,
but a false witness is deceitful.

26 Whoever fears the LORD
has a secure fortress,
and for their children it will be a refuge.

27 The fear of the LORD

is a fountain of life,
turning a person from
the snares of death.

28 A large population is a king's glory,
but without subjects a prince is ruined.

29 Whoever is patient has
great understanding,
but one who is quick-tem-
pered displays folly.

30 A heart at peace gives life to the body,
but envy rots the bones.

31 Whoever oppresses the poor
shows contempt for their Maker,
but whoever is kind to the
needy honors God.

32 When calamity comes, the
wicked are brought down,
but even in death the righ-
teous seek refuge in God.

33 Wisdom reposes in the
heart of the discerning
and even among fools she
lets herself be known.

34 Righteousness exalts a nation,
but sin condemns any people.

35 A king delights in a wise servant,
but a shameful servant arouses his fury.

Reread verse 12. When we focus more on what looks comfortable or convenient in the moment than what will happen later, we can make decisions that are well-intentioned but shortsighted. Sometimes these decisions result in temporary joy.

Now read verse 13. The NLT translation puts it, *"When the laughter ends, the grief remains."* We often realize that what seemed right at the time turned out to be ultimately unwise.

Think of a choice you've made that seemed good at first but eventually had negative repercussions. Looking back, what immediate factors did you possibly overemphasize (either positive or negative)?

What long-term outcomes did you possibly overlook?

Naturally, one way to discover the wrong choice is to make that choice and experience the consequences. We all learn important lessons this way. But growing in godly discernment means failure is not our only teacher. Through His Word and His Spirit, the Lord teaches us how to examine each path and its end *before* we take a step.

Write out Proverbs 14:4 here:

No, this isn't just ancient farming advice! When you read *manger*, think "feeding trough." The more oxen a farmer had, the nastier this trough would get and the more frequently it would require cleaning. So . . . should farmers still buy oxen? Of course! The ox's strength would be exponentially beneficial for a good harvest; it would be foolish to exchange long-term blessings for short-term convenience.

Think of an action or conversation you've avoided because it's difficult (like cleaning a trough) even though it would be good for you and others. How could you pray for discernment in this area to ensure you don't exchange long-term blessings for short-term convenience?

How might this same principle apply to spiritual disciplines like prayer and reading God's Word regularly (even when it would be easier not to)?

Read Proverbs 14:1 again and highlight, circle, or underline it. Similar to the apostle Paul's words about *"build[ing] up"* in 1 Corinthians 10:23 (ESV), this verse depicts wisdom as a construction project—one that requires patience, intentionality, and vision so all the decisions we make along the way have the final result in mind. Brick by brick, we labor for the Lord, asking Him to help us discern where and how our resources are best used to accomplish His will for our lives. When we build faithfully on His firm foundation, we'll never labor in vain.

HOW CAN I TRUST MY OWN DISCERNMENT?

As we consider what it means to discern God's will for our lives, it's important to remember that, in the words of Bible teacher Jen Wilkin, God is so much more than a "cosmic Dear Abby, a benevolent advice columnist who fields our toughest questions about relationships and circumstances."[1] Seeking His will doesn't mean asking Him for a "yes" or "no" answer about what to do in every single moment of our lives, paranoid that we'll make a mistake if we try to use the discernment He Himself has given us. *What if I get it wrong? What if I do something that can't be undone?*

Take a deep breath, friend. At the end of the day, Jesus has already told us what to do in all circumstances: *"Follow me"* (Matthew 4:19). As long as we obey this instruction first and foremost, whatever choices we make will be the right ones—and even when we disobey and mess up, God is still more than capable of getting us where we need to go.

Instead of endlessly and anxiously questioning all our choices, let's keep it simple with just a few steps:

Does this decision have a moral component?
(Is it a matter of right and wrong?)

NO

Does the decision have significant and/or long-term implications?

NO

God gives us freedom to choose!

YES

YES

Does God's Word either clearly prohibit or clearly promote one course of action in this situation?

NO

The best choice will likely be at the center of these factors:

YES

The best choice is to obey God's clear directive.

DAY 15

PROVERBS 15

The State of Your Heart Matters

Have you ever flinched at a "gotcha" scene in a suspenseful movie? You know, the kind that starts with a peaceful, tree-lined street, leaves rustling gently in the breeze—and then *boom!* An explosion right when you least expect it.

We might suspect similar scare tactics in Proverbs 15, which includes peaceful reassurances about God as well as some truths that may feel jarring. However, as we'll see, God always leads us to a healthy and holy fear of Him that doesn't cause us anxiety but rather delivers us from it.

READ AND RESPOND

PROVERBS 15

1 A gentle answer turns away wrath,
but a harsh word stirs up anger.

2 The tongue of the wise
adorns knowledge,
but the mouth of the fool gushes folly.

3 The eyes of the LORD are everywhere,
keeping watch on the
wicked and the good.

4 The soothing tongue is a tree of life,
but a perverse tongue crushes the spirit.

5 A fool spurns a parent's discipline,
but whoever heeds correc-
tion shows prudence.

6 The house of the righteous
contains great treasure,
but the income of the
wicked brings ruin.

7 The lips of the wise spread knowledge,
but the hearts of fools are not upright.

8 The LORD detests the sac-
rifice of the wicked,
but the prayer of the up-
right pleases him.

9 The LORD detests the
way of the wicked,
but he loves those who pur-
sue righteousness.

10 Stern discipline awaits any-
one who leaves the path;
the one who hates correction will die.

11 Death and Destruction lie
open before the LORD—
how much more do human hearts!

12 Mockers resent correction,
so they avoid the wise.

13 A happy heart makes the face cheerful,
but heartache crushes the spirit.

14 The discerning heart seeks knowledge,
but the mouth of a fool feeds on folly.

15 All the days of the op-
pressed are wretched,
but the cheerful heart
has a continual feast.

16 Better a little with the fear of the LORD
than great wealth with turmoil.

17 Better a small serving of
vegetables with love
than a fattened calf with hatred.

18 A hot-tempered per-
son stirs up conflict,
but the one who is pa-
tient calms a quarrel.

19 The way of the sluggard is
blocked with thorns,
but the path of the upright is a highway.

20 A wise son brings joy to his father,
but a foolish man despises his mother.

21 Folly brings joy to one
who has no sense,
but whoever has understand-
ing keeps a straight course.

22 Plans fail for lack of counsel,
but with many advisers they succeed.

23 A person finds joy in giv-
ing an apt reply—
and how good is a timely word!

24 The path of life leads up-
ward for the prudent
to keep them from going down
to the realm of the dead.

25 The LORD tears down the
house of the proud,
but he sets the widow's
boundary stones in place.

26 The LORD detests the
thoughts of the wicked,
but gracious words are pure in his sight.

27 The greedy bring ruin
to their households,
but the one who hates bribes will live.

28 The heart of the
righteous weighs its answers,
but the mouth of the
wicked gushes evil.

29 The LORD is far from the wicked,
but he hears the prayer of the righteous.

30 Light in a messenger's eyes
brings joy to the heart,
and good news gives
health to the bones.

31 Whoever heeds life-giving correction
will be at home among the wise.

32 Those who disregard
discipline despise themselves,
but the one who heeds
correction gains understanding.

33 Wisdom's instruction is
to fear the LORD,
and humility comes before honor.

Proverbs 15 begins with the comforting promise that *"the eyes of the LORD are everywhere, keeping watch on the wicked and the good"* (v. 3). This description of God may remind us of how a lonely woman named Hagar called Him *"the God who sees me"* in Genesis 16:13, or how Jesus taught in Matthew 10:29 that *"not [even] one [sparrow] will fall to the ground outside your Father's care."*

What other Bible stories or Scriptures remind you that God is all-seeing, or omniscient? How do you feel when you picture God *"keeping watch"* over you (Proverbs 15:3)?

The fact that God is all-seeing consoles and encourages us in so many ways. He bears witness to the hidden parts of us that desperately cry out to be seen.

Yet He humbles us too. *God is all-seeing!* So He beholds the sinful parts of us that we desperately want to hide. Fill in the missing portions of the verses below and take note of the consistency in God's character, His preferences, and His response to sin.

VERSE 8:

The LORD ______________________________ the __________

__________________ of the wicked, but the ______________________

of the upright __________________________ him.

VERSE 9:

The LORD ____________________ the _________________________ of the wicked,

but he ________________________ those who

__________________ ______________________.

VERSE 26:

The LORD ____________________ the _______________________ of the wicked,

but ____________________ __________________

are ____________________ in his sight.

Proverbs 15 reminds us three times that sin is *"detestable to the LORD"* (vv. 8, 9, 26).

The ESV Bible uses the word *abomination* instead of *detestable.* By itself this word feels pretty explosive—and it's rarely used today for just that reason. Still, this is a translated word that describes God's regard for the outward *"way of the wicked"* (v. 9) and the inward *"thoughts of the wicked"* (v. 26). God even rejects the *"sacrifice of the wicked"* (v. 8) because, as scholars have noted, "they offer everything except what [He] asked for: their heart."[1]

How do you feel when you consider this side of God's omniscience? Why?

As Proverbs 15:11 communicates, *"human hearts" "lie open before the LORD."* We can't shut Him out. All our walls are windows.

We sometimes think of fearing the Lord as an involuntary panic response to this fact, but let's remember something about our heavenly Father. He is not a "gotcha" God. He's not waiting to terrify us with unexpected booms of judgment; He's waiting to set us free from sin when we choose to walk with Him in humility and accountability. Rather than a convoluted route with anxiety-inducing frights at every turn,

God's path for His people is a *"level highway"* (v. 19 ESV) that leads us *"straight ahead"* (v. 21 ESV) to eternal life through faith in Jesus.

Read verses 16 and 33.

How is the reverential fear of God different from anxious fear of God?

Why is this difference so important?

We don't choose whether God sees us (He does) or what He sees (He sees everything). But knowing His eyes are on us, we can choose to live with our eyes on Him. We can pray like King David in Psalm 139:23–24,

Search me, God, and know my heart;
test me and know my anxious thoughts.
See if there is any offensive way in me,
and lead me in the way everlasting.

Let's take a moment to dig deep. Is there anything you feel afraid for God to know about you? Any ways and thoughts you fear God might find abominable if He saw them?

Friend, here's the beautiful truth: God already sees. He already knows. And He loves you more than you could ever possibly imagine. He sent His own Son, Jesus, to rescue you from sin and death forever!

Describe how this good news *"gives health to [your] bones,"* as Proverbs 15:30 says:

DAY 16

PROVERBS 16

Submit to God, Humbly

Remember those senior superlatives from your high school yearbook? Best hair. Best dressed. Cutest couple. Most athletic. Well, today's proverbs give us a few superlatives too—but they're not quite what we'd expect based on the world's ideas of popularity and success.

READ AND RESPOND

PROVERBS 16

1 To humans belong the
plans of the heart,
but from the LORD comes the
proper answer of the tongue.

2 All a person's ways seem pure to them,
but motives are weighed by the LORD.

3 Commit to the LORD whatever you do,
and he will establish your plans.

4 The LORD works out everything
to its proper end—
even the wicked for a day of disaster.

5 The LORD detests all the proud of heart.
Be sure of this: They will
not go unpunished.

6 Through love and faithfulness
sin is atoned for;
through the fear of the
LORD evil is avoided.

7 When the LORD takes
pleasure in anyone's way,
he causes their enemies to
make peace with them.

8 Better a little with righteousness
than much gain with injustice.

9 In their hearts humans plan their course,
but the LORD establishes their steps.

10 The lips of a king speak as an oracle,
and his mouth does not betray justice.

11 Honest scales and balances
belong to the LORD;
all the weights in the bag
are of his making.

12 Kings detest wrongdoing,
for a throne is established
through righteousness.

13 Kings take pleasure in honest lips;
they value the one who
speaks what is right.

14 A king's wrath is a messenger of death,
but the wise will appease it.

15 When a king's face
brightens, it means life;
his favor is like a rain cloud in spring.

16 How much better to get
wisdom than gold,
to get insight rather than silver!

17 The highway of the upright avoids evil;
those who guard their ways
preserve their lives.

18 Pride goes before destruction,
a haughty spirit before a fall.

19 Better to be lowly in spirit
along with the oppressed
than to share plunder with the proud.

20 Whoever gives heed to
instruction prospers,
and blessed is the one who
trusts in the LORD.

21 The wise in heart are called discerning,
and gracious words
promote instruction.

22 Prudence is a fountain of
life to the prudent,
but folly brings punishment to fools.

23 The hearts of the wise make
their mouths prudent,
and their lips promote instruction.

24 Gracious words are a honeycomb,
sweet to the soul and
healing to the bones.

25 There is a way that appears to be right,
but in the end it leads to death.

26 The appetite of laborers
works for them;

their hunger drives them on.

27 A scoundrel plots evil,
and on their lips it is
like a scorching fire.

28 A perverse person stirs up conflict,
and a gossip separates close friends.

29 A violent person entices their neighbor
and leads them down a
path that is not good.

30 Whoever winks with their
eye is plotting perversity;
whoever purses their lips is bent on evil.

31 Gray hair is a crown of splendor;
it is attained in the way
of righteousness.

32 Better a patient person than a warrior,
one with self-control than
one who takes a city.

33 The lot is cast into the lap,
but its every decision is from the LORD.

Let's start today's study by noting the verses in Proverbs 16 that compare two things and identify one of them as superior.

> Circle every place you find the word *better*.
>
> Now, underline or highlight what Scripture says is *"better."* The person with *"much gain"* (v. 8) and power enough to *"[take] a city"* (v. 32), a feat reserved for conquering kings in the Ancient Near East, sure sounds like they would have been voted "most likely to succeed" by their graduating class.

Yet God says all the power in the world amounts to nothing if it's obtained through injustice, greed, pride, and unrighteous anger. In fact, the lowly and anonymous people who are the *least* successful in the world's eyes are often the ones who truly prosper, leading peaceful, wise, and self-controlled lives as servants of God.

How did Jesus later elaborate on this idea in His Sermon on the Mount?

Look up and read the "Beatitudes" in Matthew 5:2–11.

Make a list of all the similarities to Proverbs 16 you read:

Circle the ways Jesus is described in the passages below:

He grew up before him like a tender shoot,
and like a root out of dry ground.
He had no beauty or majesty to attract us to him,
nothing in his appearance that we should desire him.
Isaiah 53:2

For you know the grace of our Lord Jesus Christ, that though he was rich,
yet for your sake he became poor, so that you through his poverty might become rich.
2 Corinthians 8:9

In her book *Anonymous*, Dr. Alicia Britt Chole writes,

"Our desire to 'be like Jesus' contains several exemption clauses, not the least of which are Jesus' hidden years, desert experiences, temptations, tortures, and crucifixion."[1]

What might it look like to remove these "exemptions" from our prayers and ask God to make us Christlike even through humbling circumstances and trials?

Only God's Kingdom lasts forever.

All other beauty fades. All other power shifts. All other treasures tarnish. For this reason, Proverbs 16:18 warns us against pride, or the inclination to glorify ourselves rather than God: *"Pride goes before destruction, a haughty spirit before a fall."* Remember how we learned about antithetical proverbs on Day 10 where Proverbs 10 revealed two contrasting paths?

Well, Proverbs 16:18 isn't antithetical; it's a ***synonymous proverb,*** **meaning the second half repeats the first half,** in this case emphasizing that pride always leads to the same bad outcome.

In the end, every person will bow before the Lord (Philippians 2:10), yet God graciously gives us the choice to kneel in humility rather than fall from pride. As Proverbs 16:3 says, we can *"commit to the LORD whatever [we] do, and he will establish [our] plans."*

To be sure, this is not a promise that God will execute all our plans exactly as we desire. It's actually a much better promise: As the Holy Spirit works in our hearts to make us more *"gentle and lowly"* like our Savior (Matthew 11:29 ESV), we learn to yield our best-laid plans to His perfect purposes for our lives.

What plans are you currently making that you could commit or recommit to God? (From 10-year career plans to tonight's dinner plans, He is Lord of it all!)

DAY 17

PROVERBS 17

Valuing Peace & Patience

Reading Proverbs 17 is a bit like playing a game of "Would You Rather."

Would you rather ...

> Share a meal of bread crust in a loving home or attend a delicious banquet with hostile guests (v. 1)?
>
> Receive a word of correction or have someone punch you 100 times (v. 10)?
>
> Do life with a foolish friend or shake hands with an angry mama bear (v. 12)?

If only these were merely hypothetical questions! The truth is that relationships are filled with complicated choices for everyone, including the wise.

READ AND RESPOND

PROVERBS 17

1 Better a dry crust with peace and quiet
  than a house full of feasting, with strife.

2 A prudent servant will rule
over a disgraceful son
  and will share the inheri-
tance as one of the family.

3 The crucible for silver and
the furnace for gold,
  but the Lord tests the heart.

4 A wicked person listens to deceitful lips;
  a liar pays attention to a de-
structive tongue.

5 Whoever mocks the poor shows
contempt for their Maker;
  whoever gloats over disas-
ter will not go unpunished.

6 Children's children are a
crown to the aged,

and parents are the pride
of their children.

7 Eloquent lips are
unsuited to a godless fool—
how much worse lying lips to a ruler!

8 A bribe is seen as a charm
by the one who gives it;
they think success will
come at every turn.

9 Whoever would foster love
covers over an offense,
but whoever repeats the mat-
ter separates close friends.

10 A rebuke impresses a discerning person
more than a hundred lashes a fool.

11 Evildoers foster rebellion against God;
the messenger of death will
be sent against them.

12 Better to meet a bear
robbed of her cubs
than a fool bent on folly.

13 Evil will never leave the house
of one who pays back evil for good.

14 Starting a quarrel is like
breaching a dam;
so drop the matter be-
fore a dispute breaks out.

15 Acquitting the guilty and con-
demning the innocent—
the LORD detests them both.

16 Why should fools have
money in hand to buy wisdom,
when they are not able
to understand it?

17 A friend loves at all times,
and a brother is born for
a time of adversity.

18 One who has no sense
shakes hands in pledge
and puts up security for a neighbor.

19 Whoever loves a quarrel loves sin;
whoever builds a high gate
invites destruction.

20 One whose heart is cor-
rupt does not prosper;
one whose tongue is per-
verse falls into trouble.

21 To have a fool for a child brings grief;
there is no joy for the parent of a godless fool.

22 A cheerful heart is good medicine,
but a crushed spirit dries up the bones.

23 The wicked accept bribes in secret
to pervert the course of justice.

24 A discerning person keeps wisdom in view,
but a fool's eyes wander to the ends of the earth.

25 A foolish son brings grief to his father
and bitterness to the mother who bore him.

26 If imposing a fine on the innocent is not good,
surely to flog honest officials is not right.

27 The one who has knowledge uses words with restraint,
and whoever has understanding is even-tempered.

28 Even fools are thought wise if they keep silent,
and discerning if they hold their tongues.

We don't find an instruction manual for how to have a perfect marriage, family, or friendship in Proverbs 17; however, we *do* find two **God-honoring strategies for pursuing peace and practicing patience** even when problems arise.

1. PURSUE PEACE.

Proverbs 17:14 says, *"Starting a quarrel is like breaching a dam; so drop the matter before a dispute breaks out."* Ancient readers of this proverb would have understood the metaphor here and pictured a leaky dam or reservoir; at first, water dribbles out slowly, but then the pressure builds, widening the breach and eventually causing an uncontrollable flood.

To avoid this kind of outburst in our relationships, we can peacefully address minor disagreements and difficulties before they *"break out"* into major conflicts. We can also express and release our emotions regularly instead of letting resentments accumulate in unhealthy ways. There's no danger of the dam bursting if there's no dam!

When have you built a "resentment reservoir" to hold back hard feelings in a relationship (or been in a relationship where someone did this)? What was the result?

In Proverbs 10:11, we learned *"the mouth of the righteous is a fountain of life."*

How does this contrast the metaphor of *"starting a quarrel is like a breaching of a dam"* from verse 14?

In what ways can you ensure what is coming out of your mouth will be a "fountain of life" rather than causing a "breach in a dam" that will hit the recipient with a flood of resentment or anger?

Pursuing peace with others means choosing to say what needs to be said now to avoid disaster later. And it also means *not* saying what *doesn't* need to be said. Both the first and final verses of today's reading commend a healthy holding of our tongues, saying, *"The one who has knowledge uses words with restraint . . . is even-tempered"* (Proverbs 17:27).

Let's think back to our discussion of discernment on Day 14. How does godly discernment help us know what to speak up about and what to let go as peacemakers in our relationships?

2. PRACTICE PATIENCE.

In today's reading, Proverbs 17:9 also advises that *"whoever would foster love covers over an offense."* Interestingly, the word *covers* can also be translated as *"conceals"* (CSB, NASB). Is God asking us to hide our hurt and sweep sin under the rug in the name of loving others?

Definitely not!

What does Proverbs 17:15 say about *"acquitting the guilty and condemning the innocent"* (i.e., denying the reality of their wrongdoing)?

Covering offenses does not mean living in denial. But much like God patiently *"made garments of skin for Adam and his wife and clothed them"* after they sinned against Him in Eden (Genesis 3:21), the covering in Proverbs 17:9 emphasizes privately, respectfully confronting one another when necessary rather than publicly complaining.

In what other ways did God demonstrate patience toward Adam and Eve despite their offense (Genesis 3:8–24)? How has He shown patience toward you?

Which relationship in your life tests your patience the most? What does Proverbs 17:9 tell us to *"foster,"* and how can you do that today in this relationship?

DAY 18

PROVERBS 18

Wise Community Safeguards Against Foolishness

You may have heard the saying that "it takes a village to raise a child." Though no one knows its exact origins, there are similar idioms in some African cultures; for instance, the Bantu proverb *omwana takulila nju emoi* means "a child does not grow up only in a single home."

In today's Scriptures, we see there are many things "it takes a village" to do. In fact, there isn't much God asks us to do or decide alone.

READ AND RESPOND

PROVERBS 18

1 An unfriendly person
pursues selfish ends
  and against all sound
judgment starts quarrels.

2 Fools find no pleasure in understanding
  but delight in airing
their own opinions.

3 When wickedness comes,
so does contempt,
  and with shame comes reproach.

4 The words of the mouth
are deep waters,
  but the fountain of wisdom
is a rushing stream.

5 It is not good to be partial to the wicked
  and so deprive the innocent of justice.

6 The lips of fools bring them strife,
  and their mouths invite a beating.

7 The mouths of fools are their undoing,
  and their lips are a snare
to their very lives.

8 The words of a gossip are
like choice morsels;
  they go down to the inmost parts.

9 One who is slack in his work
is brother to one who destroys.

10 The name of the LORD
is a fortified tower;
the righteous run to it and are safe.

11 The wealth of the rich is
their fortified city;
they imagine it a wall too high to scale.

12 Before a downfall the heart is haughty,
but humility comes before honor.

13 To answer before listening—
that is folly and shame.

14 The human spirit can
endure in sickness,
but a crushed spirit who can bear?

15 The heart of the discerning
acquires knowledge,
for the ears of the wise seek it out.

16 A gift opens the way
and ushers the giver into
the presence of the great.

17 In a lawsuit the first to
speak seems right,
until someone comes forward
and cross-examines.

18 Casting the lot settles disputes
and keeps strong opponents apart.

19 A brother wronged is more
unyielding than a fortified city;
disputes are like the barred
gates of a citadel.

20 From the fruit of their mouth
a person's stomach is filled;
with the harvest of their
lips they are satisfied.

21 The tongue has the power
of life and death,
and those who love it will eat its fruit.

22 He who finds a wife finds what is good
and receives favor from the LORD.

23 The poor plead for mercy,
but the rich answer harshly.

24 One who has unreliable
friends soon comes to ruin,
but there is a friend who
sticks closer than a brother.

Read Proverbs 18:1 again. What might be some dangers of withdrawing from "village" life (community, accountability, church fellowship, etc.)? What kinds of choices do people tend to make in isolation?

None of us has *only* good ideas *all* the time. But if there's no "village" around us to lovingly challenge our not-so-great ideas, they're more likely to become not-so-great choices. Perhaps this is one reason why God said in Genesis 2:18, after creating the first human (Adam) but before creating the second human (Eve), *"It is not good that the man should be alone"* (ESV). We risk making regrettable decisions when we speak or act without a willingness to hear from others (Proverbs 18:13).

Record how the person in each of the following verses seeks knowledge or understanding. Circle or highlight the greatest distinctions you see.

PROVERBS 18:15	PROVERBS 18:2

Just as a case in court seems right until the cross-examination begins (Proverbs 18:17), our own ideas benefit from being tested by those we trust. It takes humility to let others question our plans, but that discomfort is a small price to pay for trading ill-conceived impulses for wise choices.

The Hebrew word for *"cross-examine,"* חָקַר (*chaqar*), used in verse 17 also appears in Deuteronomy 13:14 where God commanded His people to *"inquire, probe and investigate"* any hidden sin in their community and get rid of it for everyone's benefit.

Who in your "village" (godly friends, family, church members, etc.) could help you examine an upcoming decision? How could you do the same for them?

Now let's compare the *cross-examining* in Proverbs 18:17 to the *disputing* in verse 19. What's the difference? What are some ways to ensure that examining doesn't turn into quarreling?

Proverbs 18:18 offers perhaps unexpected advice about conflict resolution: *"Casting the lot settles disputes and keeps strong opponents apart."* Lot casting was an ancient decision-making method similar to flipping a coin or rolling dice, which was considered fair and unbiased since whoever rolled the dice (so to speak) couldn't control the outcome.

So, should we all grab the nearest Yahtzee next time we have a choice to make? Not quite. The main idea here is that endless deliberation or dispute over any decision is unproductive, so in a gridlock, as David Guzik observes, "appealing to an outside authority" can be helpful. "In this case, the outside authority is the casting of lots, but the principle can be applied to other agreed-upon authorities," advisers, or mediators.[1] We don't have to do it alone.

When you feel overwhelmed by pressure to make the right decision, how might it help you to remember that you don't have to do it alone?

Return to and read Proverbs 16:33. What does it say about casting lots, and how does this lift some of the burden of decision-making off our shoulders?

DAY 19

PROVERBS 19

Wisdom Must Be Continuously Pursued

Throughout our study, the book of Proverbs has encouraged us to pursue the practical and spiritual benefits of wisdom. Now we'll consider the dangers of growing complacent in our pursuit. In today's reading, Solomon used exaggeration to make a point—and maybe even to make us smile. But the lesson we learn about apathy isn't a laughing matter.

READ AND RESPOND

PROVERBS 19

1 Better the poor whose walk is blameless
than a fool whose lips are perverse.

2 Desire without knowledge
is not good—
how much more will hasty
feet miss the way!

3 A person's own folly leads to their ruin,
yet their heart rages against the LORD.

4 Wealth attracts many friends,
but even the closest friend of
the poor person deserts them.

5 A false witness will not go unpunished,
and whoever pours out
lies will not go free.

6 Many curry favor with a ruler,
and everyone is the friend
of one who gives gifts.

7 The poor are shunned by
all their relatives—
how much more do their
friends avoid them!

Though the poor pursue
them with pleading,
they are nowhere to be found.

8 The one who gets wisdom loves life;
the one who cherishes

understanding will soon prosper.

9 A false witness will not go unpunished,
and whoever pours out lies will perish.

10 It is not fitting for a fool
to live in luxury—
how much worse for a slave
to rule over princes!

11 A person's wisdom yields patience;
it is to one's glory to
overlook an offense.

12 A king's rage is like the roar of a lion,
but his favor is like dew on the grass.

13 A foolish child is a father's ruin,
and a quarrelsome wife is like
the constant dripping of a leaky roof.

14 Houses and wealth are
inherited from parents,
but a prudent wife is from the LORD.

15 Laziness brings on deep sleep,
and the shiftless go hungry.

16 Whoever keeps commandments
keeps their life,
but whoever shows contempt
for their ways will die.

17 Whoever is kind to the
poor lends to the LORD,
and he will reward them
for what they have done.

18 Discipline your children,
for in that there is hope;
do not be a willing party to their death.

19 A hot-tempered person
must pay the penalty;
rescue them, and you will
have to do it again.

20 Listen to advice and accept discipline,
and at the end you will be
counted among the wise.

21 Many are the plans in a person's heart,
but it is the LORD's
purpose that prevails.

22 What a person desires is unfailing love;
better to be poor than a liar.

23 The fear of the LORD leads to life;
then one rests content,
untouched by trouble.

24 A sluggard buries his hand in the dish;
he will not even bring it
back to his mouth!

25 Flog a mocker, and the simple
will learn prudence;
rebuke the discerning, and
they will gain knowledge.

26 Whoever robs their father
and drives out their mother
is a child who brings
shame and disgrace.
27 Stop listening to instruction, my son,
and you will stray from the
words of knowledge.

28 A corrupt witness mocks at justice,
and the mouth of the
wicked gulps down evil.

29 Penalties are prepared for mockers,
and beatings for the backs of fools.

In verse 15, we meet a person who is hungry because he stayed in bed rather than going to work. His lack of food is the outcome of idleness. Nine verses later, we encounter someone who's taken slothfulness to a ludicrous extreme: This person isn't hungry because he lacks food but because he lacks motivation to move his hand from the dish in front of him to his own mouth (v. 24).

Solomon's comical hyperbole illustrates how laziness can spiral into a colossal calamity, which prods us to take inventory of our own spiritual grit. Much like the sluggard's bowl of food, we have the nourishment of God's Word at our fingertips, but it's up to us to consume it.

What, if anything, keeps you from "feeding" yourself spiritually?

On the other hand, what motivates you to keep investing in your relationship with God?

Interestingly, tucked between Solomon's outlandish illustrations of slothfulness (vv. 15, 24) is a call to generosity: *"Whoever is kind to the poor lends to the Lord, and he will reward them for what they have done"* (v. 17).

In this context, *"the poor"* doesn't just refer to people lacking money. **The Hebrew word used here דַּל (*dal*) means *"low, weak, poor, thin"*; meanwhile the word kind חָנַן (*Chanan*) means *"to be gracious, to show favor or mercy."*** In other translations, *kind* is translated "generous." Proverbs—like Scripture as a whole—consistently commends deep concern for the needs of the poor (Proverbs 14:21; Proverbs 19:7; Proverbs 21:13; Proverbs 29:7), yet Solomon's mandate encompasses more than financial benevolence. It describes the attitude God wants us to have toward the vulnerable in our midst.

We may not always have extra money to give to those in need, but even so, we all have something to share. Perhaps it's time, talents, a listening ear, or a word of encouragement.

Think of the poor or vulnerable in your own community. What is one way you can respond to others' needs with generosity?

Proverbs 19:17 doesn't just encourage kind or generous living; it also reveals God's response to our compassionate giving. "The implication of the term 'lend' suggests that God will repay those who are generous—not necessarily with earthly wealth, but in spiritual blessing."[1]

Read Matthew 25:34–40:

"Then the King will say to those on his right, 'Come, you who are blessed by my Father; take your inheritance, the kingdom prepared for you since the creation of the world. 35 For I was hungry and you gave me something to eat, I was thirsty and you gave me something to drink, I was a stranger and you invited me in, 36 I needed clothes and you clothed me, I was sick and you looked after me, I was in prison and you came to visit me.' 37 "Then the righteous will answer him, 'Lord, when did we see you hungry and feed you, or thirsty and give you something to drink? 38 When did we see you a stranger and invite you in, or needing clothes and clothe you? 39 When did we see you sick or in prison and go to visit you?' 40 "The King will reply, 'Truly I tell you, whatever you did for one of the least of these brothers and sisters of mine, you did for me.'"

How do Jesus' words echo Solomon's in Proverbs 19:17?

How do these verses challenge or encourage you?

The generosity Jesus describes isn't an "I'll help you if you help me" exchange. It's selfless kindness with no strings attached.

In Proverbs 19:22, Solomon captured the motivation for godly generosity by saying, *"What a person desires is unfailing love."* The phrase *"unfailing love,"* or in other translations, *"steadfast love,"* comes from the Hebrew word *hesed*. It's a difficult concept to translate into English because its depth can't be captured with one word alone.

According to Bible scholar Darrell L. Bock, "*Hesed* is wrapping up in itself all the positive attributes of God: love, covenant faithfulness, mercy, grace, kindness, loyalty—in short, acts of devotion and loving-kindness that go beyond the requirements of duty."[2]

Have you ever received a gift you didn't expect? Help you couldn't repay? Kindness you didn't deserve? That's *hesed*.

Romans 5:8 describes one great act of loving-kindness we've all received from God. Write this verse below and thank God for His extravagant generosity in a short prayer.

God wants us to be marked by *"unfailing love"* (Proverbs 19:22) because it points others to His heart. And in the process, it transforms ours too. One act of kindness at a time, we become more like the One who generously gave us everything—even His very life (Philippians 2:5–11; John 3:16; Ephesians 1:3).

DAY 20

PROVERBS 20

Wisdom Develops Keen Judgment

Have you ever met someone you thought was trustworthy but then learned your first impression was wrong?

Solomon knew how difficult it can be to figure out people's true intentions. Proverbs 20 is full of practical insight about reading situations wisely, testing appearances, and recognizing character. As you read, look for the everyday moments where wisdom—or foolishness—quietly reveals itself.

READ AND RESPOND

PROVERBS 20

1 Wine is a mocker and beer a brawler;
whoever is led astray by
them is not wise.

2 A king's wrath strikes ter-
ror like the roar of a lion;
those who anger him forfeit their lives.

3 It is to one's honor to avoid strife,
but every fool is quick to quarrel.

4 Sluggards do not plow in season;
so at harvest time they
look but find nothing.

5 The purposes of a person's
heart are deep waters,
but one who has in-
sight draws them out.

6 Many claim to have unfailing love,
but a faithful person who can find?

7 The righteous lead blameless lives;
blessed are their children after them.

8 When a king sits on his throne to judge,
he winnows out all evil with his eyes.

9 Who can say, "I have
kept my heart pure;
I am clean and without sin"?

10 Differing weights and dif-
fering measures—
the LORD detests them both.

11 Even small children are
known by their actions,
so is their conduct
really pure and upright?

12 Ears that hear and eyes that see—
the LORD has made them both.

13 Do not love sleep or
you will grow poor;
stay awake and you will
have food to spare.

14 "It's no good, it's no good!"
says the buyer—
then goes off and boasts
about the purchase.

15 Gold there is, and rubies in abundance,
but lips that speak knowl-
edge are a rare jewel.

16 Take the garment of one who
puts up security for a stranger;
hold it in pledge if it is
done for an outsider.

17 Food gained by fraud tastes sweet,
but one ends up with a
mouth full of gravel.

18 Plans are established by seeking advice;
so if you wage war, obtain guidance.

19 A gossip betrays a confidence;
so avoid anyone who talks too much.

20 If someone curses their fa-
ther or mother,
their lamp will be snuffed
out in pitch darkness.

21 An inheritance claimed too soon
will not be blessed at the end.

22 Do not say, "I'll pay you
back for this wrong!"
Wait for the LORD, and
he will avenge you.

23 The LORD detests differing weights,
and dishonest scales do not please him.

24 A person's steps are di-
rected by the LORD.
How then can anyone un-
derstand their own way?

25 It is a trap to dedicate something rashly
and only later to consider one's vows.

26 A wise king winnows out the wicked;
he drives the
threshing wheel over them.

27 The human spirit is the
lamp of the Lord
that sheds light on one's inmost being.

28 Love and faithfulness keep a king safe;
through love his throne is made secure.

29 The glory of young men
is their strength,
gray hair the splendor of the old.

30 Blows and wounds scrub away evil,
and beatings purge the inmost being.

Read 1 Kings 3:16–28 with Proverbs 20:5 in mind. How did Solomon draw out the purposes of the heart in this situation?

Proverbs 20:8 depicts a king discerning good from evil as he seeks to make decisions rooted in justice and godliness. The image of the winnowing king implies the importance of paying attention to character, not just appearances, in our interactions with others. Disingenuous intentions aren't always obvious at first glance, but just as the threshing wheel sifts the chaff from the wheat, so wise judgment helps us sort illusion from reality.

To be clear, godly wisdom never makes us *judgmental* (Matthew 7:1–5)—if anything, the wiser we grow, the more we recognize the waywardness of our own hearts (Proverbs 20:9)!—but wisdom does make us *judicious* like the king in verse 8. He looks out from his throne and sees good and evil. He is perceptive and has moral insight.

Read Jesus' words in Matthew 7:1–5 and 15–20. How do these verses help you determine the difference between being judgmental and being judicious?

Like Jesus, Proverbs 20 recommends conduct as a wise gauge for character. No one's perfect, of course, but our behavior often reveals the attitudes of our hearts. And we can ask the Holy Spirit to alert us to any insincerity in ourselves or in others that could misguide or harm us.

Proverbs 20:6 says, *"Many claim to have unfailing love, but a faithful person who can find?"*

This rhetorical question makes sense when we understand what Solomon means by *"faithful"*: consistent in what one *says* and *does*.

> Are there any areas of your life where your words and ways may be misaligned? If so, take a moment to confess that discrepancy to the Lord, and ask Him to help you be a person marked by faithfulness.

Even as we grow in good judgment, our discernment is imperfect. That's why seeking counsel, as long as we're selective about *who* we consult (vv. 18–19), is often a wise move.

> Does your go-to process for making decisions usually involve seeking counsel? From whom?

> How could you apply Proverbs 20:18–19 to a decision you're facing right now?

When it comes to discernment, we may wonder, *If I make a bad decision, will I wreck God's plan for me?*

Thankfully, God isn't bound by human timelines or constricted by human perceptions, so we may not always understand what He's doing, but Scripture assures us He's working everything out for our good and His glory (Romans 8:28). In the end, His purposes will prevail (Proverbs 19:21). That's why our best decision every day is to get to know God intimately so we can trust Him—and His plans—completely.

If you need more fodder to fuel your trust, Proverbs 20:28 contains a poignant picture of God's character. Do you recognize the phrase *"unfailing love"* (NLT)? Once again, the Hebrew word *hesed* (see Day 19) reminds us who God is. His kindness and grace are extravagant, His devotion unshakeable. Not only is His throne secure, but His heart is unchanging. Because He rules and reigns as a perfect King, we can put our faith in His faithfulness

DAY 21

PROVERBS 21

The Lord Delights in Righteousness & Justice

"Two Truths and a Lie" is a group game with a simple premise: You share two things about yourself that are true and one that isn't, and then everyone tries to guess the untruth. If your lie goes undetected, you win.

While a lie may secure the victory in this game, it's a sure path to losing in real life. In today's reading, we'll look at a type of lying that's especially hard to address—deceiving ourselves.

READ AND RESPOND

PROVERBS 21

1 In the LORD's hand the king's
heart is a stream of water
that he channels toward
all who please him.

2 A person may think their
own ways are right,
but the LORD weighs the heart.

3 To do what is right and just
is more acceptable to the
LORD than sacrifice.

4 Haughty eyes and a proud heart—
the unplowed field of the
wicked—produce sin.

5 The plans of the diligent lead to profit
as surely as haste leads to poverty.

6 A fortune made by a lying tongue
is a fleeting vapor and a deadly snare.

7 The violence of the wicked
will drag them away,
for they refuse to do what is right.

8 The way of the guilty is devious,
but the conduct of the
innocent is upright.

9 Better to live on a corner of the roof
than share a house with
a quarrelsome wife.

10 The wicked crave evil;
their neighbors get no
mercy from them.

11 When a mocker is punished,
the simple gain wisdom;
by paying attention to the
wise they get knowledge.

12 The Righteous One takes note
of the house of the wicked
and brings the wicked to ruin.

13 Whoever shuts their ears
to the cry of the poor
will also cry out and not be answered.

14 A gift given in secret soothes anger,
and a bribe concealed in the
cloak pacifies great wrath.

15 When justice is done, it
brings joy to the righteous
but terror to evildoers.

16 Whoever strays from the
path of prudence
comes to rest in the
company of the dead.

17 Whoever loves pleasure
will become poor;
whoever loves wine and olive
oil will never be rich.

18 The wicked become a
ransom for the righteous,
and the unfaithful for the upright.

19 Better to live in a desert
than with a quarrelsome
and nagging wife.

20 The wise store up choice
food and olive oil,
but fools gulp theirs down.

21 Whoever pursues
righteousness and love
finds life, prosperity and honor.

22 One who is wise can go up
against the city of the mighty
and pull down the stronghold
in which they trust.

23 Those who guard their
mouths and their tongues

keep themselves from calamity.

24 The proud and arrogant
person—"Mocker" is his name—
behaves with insolent fury.

25 The craving of a sluggard
will be the death of him,
because his hands refuse to work.
26 All day long he craves for more,
but the righteous give without sparing.

27 The sacrifice of the
wicked is detestable—
how much more so when
brought with evil intent!

28 A false witness will perish,
but a careful listener will
testify successfully.

29 The wicked put up a bold front,
but the upright give
thought to their ways.

30 There is no wisdom, no insight, no plan
that can succeed against the LORD.

31 The horse is made ready
for the day of battle,
but victory rests with the LORD.

Proverbs 21:4 warns that "haughty eyes" and a "proud heart" can lead to sin. Sadly, pride can lead to self-righteousness, which makes us blind to our sin, or quick to explain it away with half-truths or faulty explanations.

What kind of lies have you told yourself? How have you perhaps deceived yourself by avoiding difficult truths or overlooking your own sin at times?

Thank God that Proverbs 21:2 reminds us that even if we can't tell the difference between the truths and lies in our own hearts, God can. And if we ask Him, He'll show us what He sees.

Solomon may have learned the truth of Proverbs 21:2 from his own father, King David, who discovered how quickly a deceived heart can drive bad decisions (read 2 Samuel 11–12 for the whole story).

Look up and read Psalm 139:1–18, 23–24. Compare Solomon's words in Proverbs 21 with David's in this psalm.

What pieces of David's prayer could you "borrow" as you talk with God about your own heart?

The idea of righteousness is a common theme in Proverbs 21 (and the whole book of Proverbs!), but it can feel elusive. Thankfully, verse 2 and verse 10 simplify it by reminding us that walking in righteousness starts with getting our hearts right with God. When our hearts are awry, we lose our way (Proverbs 4:23).

Sometimes it's tempting to skip this necessary heart work and focus only on doing the right things for God. But according to today's reading, God isn't impressed by a right thing done with a wrong motive.

Go back through the chapter, underlining or noting every reference to *"heart," "way," "craves"* or *"craving,"* or *"desire."* What picture begins to form about what God is paying attention to?

Now, let's read 1 Samuel 15:22:

But Samuel replied:

"Does the LORD delight in burnt offerings and sacrifices
as much as in obeying the LORD?
To obey is better than sacrifice,
and to heed is better than the fat of rams."

Compare Proverbs 21:3–4 with the passage from 1 Samuel. What message do these verses share?

Why do you think that is?

Proverbs 21:3 seems to summarize what's important to God. The word *sacrifice* here is a reference to the burnt offerings people once brought God to make atonement or cover their sins. It was also possible, and even desirable, to make offerings as an expression of gratitude. God's intent behind creating this practice in the Old Testament had less to do with *what* was offered (the animal) than *how* it was given (the motivation of the heart).

Thanks to the perfect sacrifice of Jesus, we no longer have to mend our relationship with God through burnt offerings (Hebrews 10:12–14). But we are still wise to apply the message of Proverbs 21:3–4 to our own lives. Doing what is right from a pure and sincere heart has always been God's desire for His people.

Can you identify any way you may be "going through the motions" for God without a spirit of gratitude and love? If so, how could you ask God to help you change?

HOW I AM "GOING THROUGH THE MOTIONS"	HOW I WILL ASK GOD TO "HELP ME CHANGE"

Proverbs 21 ends with "snapshots" of life that show us how to *"do what is right and just"* (v. 3) as we navigate relationships and responsibilities. According to these verses, everyday righteousness looks like practicing patience and honesty (vv. 5, 6, 28), being fair and generous (vv. 7, 26), offering mercy and caring for the poor (vv. 10, 13), refusing to quarrel (v. 19), practicing kindness (v. 21), speaking wisely and listening well (vv. 23, 28), and remaining humble and teachable (vv. 11, 24).

Consider a "snapshot" of your daily life. Where do you see righteousness displayed? Write about it or draw it here:

If what you see in your life doesn't look like the snapshot in Proverbs 21, remember where righteousness begins. Keep talking to God about what's going on in your heart. He loves you as you are and is committed to helping you grow into who you were created to be!

DAY 22

PROVERBS 22

Practicing Practical Wisdom & Avoiding Folly

When it comes to who has what—from earthly possessions to heavenly blessings—it seems we often notice differences more quickly than commonalities.

As you read Proverbs 22, pay attention to the two different ways of living constantly being described. Consider the ways you see yourself and the ways you see "others" and how Solomon wants us to see ourselves potentially in both.

READ AND RESPOND

PROVERBS 22

1 A good name is more desirable
than great riches;
to be esteemed is better
than silver or gold.

2 Rich and poor have this in common:
The LORD is the Maker of them all.

3 The prudent see danger and take refuge,
but the simple keep going
and pay the penalty.

4 Humility is the fear of the LORD;
its wages are riches and honor and life.

5 In the paths of the wicked
are snares and pitfalls,
but those who would preserve
their life stay far from them.

6 Start children off on the
way they should go,
and even when they are old
they will not turn from it.

7 The rich rule over the poor,
and the borrower is slave to the lender.

8 Whoever sows injustice reaps calamity,
and the rod they wield in

fury will be broken.

9 The generous will themselves be blessed,
for they share their food with the poor.

10 Drive out the mocker,
and out goes strife;
quarrels and insults are ended.

11 One who loves a pure heart
and who speaks with grace
will have the king for a friend.

12 The eyes of the LORD keep
watch over knowledge,
but he frustrates the words
of the unfaithful.

13 The sluggard says, "There's
a lion outside!
I'll be killed in the public square!"

14 The mouth of an adulterous
woman is a deep pit;
a man who is under the
LORD's wrath falls into it.

15 Folly is bound up in the
heart of a child,
but the rod of discipline
will drive it far away.

16 One who oppresses the poor
to increase his wealth
and one who gives gifts to the
rich—both come to poverty.

THIRTY SAYINGS OF THE WISE

Saying 1

17 Pay attention and turn your
ear to the sayings of the wise;
apply your heart to what I teach,
18 for it is pleasing when you
keep them in your heart
and have all of them ready on your lips.
19 So that your trust may be in the LORD,
I teach you today, even you.
20 Have I not written thirty
sayings for you,
sayings of counsel and knowledge,
21 teaching you to be honest
and to speak the truth,
so that you bring back truthful reports
to those you serve?

Saying 2

22 Do not exploit the poor
because they are poor
and do not crush the needy in court,
23 for the LORD will take up their case
and will exact life for life.

Saying 3
24 Do not make friends with
a hot-tempered person,
  do not associate with
one easily angered,
25 or you may learn their ways
  and get yourself ensnared.

Saying 4
26 Do not be one who shakes
hands in pledge
  or puts up security for debts;
27 if you lack the means to pay,
  your very bed will be
snatched from under you.

Saying 5
28 Do not move an ancient
boundary stone
  set up by your ancestors.

Saying 6
29 Do you see someone
skilled in their work?
  They will serve before kings;
  they will not serve before
officials of low rank.

One-third of Proverbs 22 has to do with possessions: silver and gold (v. 1), riches (vv. 1, 4, 7, 16), poverty (vv. 2, 7, 9, 16, 22), borrowing and lending (v. 7), robbery (vv. 22–23), security and debt (v. 26), and payment (v. 27). Yet Proverbs 22:2 begins with a challenge to look for common ground.

Compare Proverbs 22:2 to Genesis 1:27 and Genesis 1:31 in the chart below.

What do all of us, rich and poor, have in common?

PROVERBS 22:2	GENESIS 1:27	ROMANS 3:23

Because God is our Maker and none of us is worthy apart from Him, we are more similar than different (Romans 3:10–12; Psalm 14:3). Perhaps what Proverbs 22 is helping us define is how our actions and daily responses align or differentiate us from right living, righteousness in the image of God, and wrong living, folly in rebellion to God.

Think about all the ways your daily life is aligning with God and in what ways you are still rebelling. Don't be afraid of your responses. The grace of God is sufficient for you, and He offers us these words of wisdom in generous offering of help (2 Corinthians 12:9). Fill in the following chart:

WAYS I AM ALIGNING WITH GOD	WAYS I AM STILL REBELLING

As we read through Proverbs, it is easy to feel a bit overwhelmed or convicted. Take heart—these words are not meant or intended to be received and acted upon all at once, all the time. Proverbs 22 approaches the offering of Solomon's wisdom for very practical, everyday use. As we will learn, his words are generous and tender to the seeking heart. Let's approach this proverb with the heart of Matthew 5:6: *"Blessed are those who hunger and thirst for righteousness, for they will be filled."*

The first distinction between people in alignment and people who are still rebelling that Solomon makes is found in verse 3. While most of us do not typically describe others or ourselves as *prudent*, prudence is historically considered to be a Christian virtue, and it is here that Solomon begins his comparison.

Prudence, otherwise known as practical wisdom, helps us make choices today that protect us from trouble tomorrow. The Greek word we get prudence from is phronesis: understanding (which leads to right action), practical wisdom, prudence.[1] The Hebrew word for prudence used in Proverbs 22 is **עָרוּם**

(*arum*), meaning "shrewd, crafty, sensible, discerning, pertaining to wisdom and shrewdness in the management of affairs."[2]

Let's take a look at all the forms of practical wisdom in Proverbs 22. Return to pages 129–131 and highlight every adjective or descriptive phrasing that describes a person practicing prudence, good sense, or discernment.

By contrast, verse 3 also shows us the actions of one who is lacking prudence being simple, unsensible, or naive. The Hebrew word **פְּתִי** (*peti*) used is translated "simple, naïve, showing lack of wisdom or understanding."[3] Charles Bridges defines the *"simple"* in this verse as one who is "so absorbed in what he's doing that he is oblivious to what's coming or what's happening around him."[4] On the contrary, the prudent individual is someone who *"sees danger"* (v. 3) and pays attention to wisdom when it prompts him to go or stop, to turn around or trust.

How would you rate your own practice of prudence, using both the definition and the descriptive words you highlighted?

SPIRITUALLY DULL

SPIRITUALLY ACUTE

In what specific ways or daily circumstances might you look to using practical wisdom and embodying more of the character traits of a sensible, discerning person when making decisions?

If you're frustrated by your self-assessment, keep in mind it takes time to internalize patterns of wisdom. Hebrews 5:14 says, *"But solid food is for the mature, who by constant use have trained themselves to distinguish good from evil."*

The blessing in Proverbs is that we are immediately given applicable ways to live, respond, discern, and experience a godly life. Proverbs 22:17–29 offers the first six of thirty sayings (the remaining sayings span Proverbs 23 and 24).

Read verses 17–21 and write down what Solomon says the purpose of these sayings is.

In light of what we have learned about the practical application of wisdom in our lives, and now how Solomon intends for us to understand the purpose of these instructions, make two lists below of all the ways this proverb has taught you the benefits of practicing wisdom and the consequences of lacking it.

BENEFITS OF PRACTICING WISDOM	CONSEQUENCES OF LACKING WISDOM

Let's end today in a short time of prayer thanking God for making so clear and accessible His help and instruction for our daily living. Thank Him for any correction He may have offered through these verses and praise Him for understanding exactly where you are, at all times.

DAY 23

PROVERBS 23

Fear of the Lord Is Protection

"Are you still watching?"

If you've ever zoned out in front of the TV with a bag of chips and the latest season of your favorite Netflix show, letting the episodes auto-play for hours without picking up the remote, maybe you've seen this question pop up on your screen. At first it's just annoying—*Yes, I'm watching!*—but it might prompt a moment's pause as we realize we've been so passive that Netflix can't tell if we're still the room.

Oops. Is this something we should feel convicted about?

READ AND RESPOND

PROVERBS 23

Saying 7

1 When you sit to dine with a ruler,
note well what is before you,
2 and put a knife to your throat
if you are given to gluttony.
3 Do not crave his delicacies,
for that food is deceptive.

Saying 8

4 Do not wear yourself out to get rich;
do not trust your own cleverness.
5 Cast but a glance at riches,
and they are gone,
for they will surely sprout wings
and fly off to the sky like an eagle.

Saying 9

6 Do not eat the food of
a begrudging host,
do not crave his delicacies;
7 for he is the kind of person
who is always thinking about the cost.
"Eat and drink," he says to you,
but his heart is not with you.
8 You will vomit up the
little you have eaten
and will have wasted
your compliments.

Saying 10

9 Do not speak to fools,

for they will scorn your prudent words.

Saying 11

10 Do not move an ancient
boundary stone
or encroach on the fields
of the fatherless,
11 for their Defender is strong;
he will take up their case against you.

Saying 12

12 Apply your heart to instruction
and your ears to words of knowledge.

Saying 13

13 Do not withhold discipline
from a child;
if you punish them with the
rod, they will not die.
14 Punish them with the rod
and save them from death.

Saying 14

15 My son, if your heart is wise,
then my heart will be glad indeed;
16 my inmost being will rejoice
when your lips speak what is right.

Saying 15

17 Do not let your heart envy sinners,
but always be zealous for
the fear of the LORD.
18 There is surely a future hope for you,
and your hope will not be cut off.

Saying 16

19 Listen, my son, and be wise,
and set your heart on the right path:
20 Do not join those who
drink too much wine
or gorge themselves on meat,
21 for drunkards and
gluttons become poor,
and drowsiness clothes them in rags.

Saying 17

22 Listen to your father, who gave you life,
and do not despise your
mother when she is old.
23 Buy the truth and do not sell it—
wisdom, instruction and insight as well.
24 The father of a righteous
child has great joy;
a man who fathers a wise
son rejoices in him.
25 May your father and mother rejoice;
may she who gave you birth be joyful!

Saying 18

26 My son, give me your heart
and let your eyes delight in my ways,
27 for an adulterous woman is a deep pit,

and a wayward wife is a narrow well.
28 Like a bandit she lies in wait
and multiplies the
unfaithful among men.

Saying 19

29 Who has woe? Who has sorrow?
Who has strife? Who has complaints?
Who has needless bruises?
Who has bloodshot eyes?
30 Those who linger over wine,
who go to sample bowls of mixed wine.
31 Do not gaze at wine when it is red,
when it sparkles in the cup,
when it goes down smoothly!
32 In the end it bites like a snake
and poisons like a viper.
33 Your eyes will see strange sights,
and your mind will imagine
confusing things.
34 You will be like one sleeping
on the high seas,
lying on top of the rigging.
35 "They hit me," you will
say, "but I'm not hurt!
They beat me, but I don't feel it!
When will I wake up
so I can find another drink?"

Proverbs 23 helps us think through this question of how to exercise self-control in our intake of the world's output. Obviously, Netflix wasn't around in ancient Israel, but overindulgence was. As humans, we're all consumers and are *"given to gluttony,"* as verse 2 says—not only for food but for wealth and property (vv. 4, 10), pleasure and entertainment (vv. 30–35), sexual gratification (v. 27), and more.

In what areas of life do you find it difficult to control your appetites or practice moderation? Try completing the following statements:

- Sometimes I spend too much time or money on ______________________.
- Once I start ______________________, I find it hard to stop.
- I lose my patience if I have to wait for ______________________.
- Sometimes I think, *I must have another* ______________________ (Proverbs 23:35).

Certain appetites mentioned in Proverbs 23 intersect with needs that are not optional for us. We need money, for example, to provide for ourselves—though we don't need to weary ourselves with trying to become rich (v. 4). We also need food to eat, so when verse 2 says *"put a knife to your throat if you are given to gluttony,"* it can't mean hunger itself is punishable. Instead, we might compare this figure of speech to the English idiom "bite your tongue"—an image of thoughtful restraint that guards against excess.[1]

Write down a few examples of how God-honoring self-control might look different in each of the following contexts in your life:

- Things you *can't* refuse on a basic level (like food, funds, etc.).

- Things you *can* refuse but aren't *required* to ("extras" like dessert, entertainment, etc.).

- Things you should *always* refuse (sin, or what could lead to sin).

According to Titus 2:11–13, what trains God's people to have self-control? What *"blessed hope"* motivates us?

Proverbs 23:4 tells us one key to moderation and self-control: *"Do not wear yourself out."* In other words, know when to stop or desist. When it comes to sin, the time to stop is before we ever start doing what we know is wrong. But in matters of personal discernment, the time to stop may be when we've reached the limit of our busy schedule, the limit of our budget, or, yes, the limit of our "screen time" for the day.

We see the opposite of desisting in Proverbs 23:29–30: *"Who has woe? Who has sorrow? . . . Those who linger over wine."* The Hebrew word translated as *"linger"* is **מְאַחֲרֵי** (*m'acharey*). It means *"to remain behind, tarry, delay, be late or stay."*[2] This reminds us that making impulsive, hurried decisions is unwise—but so is lingering indecisively in places where we're tempted to overindulge.

What do you think is the difference between *"linger[ing],"* which verse 30 warns against, and *"note[ing] well what is before you,"* which verse 1 recommends?

Circle which you tend to be more like:

IMPULSIVE INDECISIVE

How does Proverbs 23 encourage you to grow in self-control either by slowing down to choose more carefully or by setting clear boundaries to avoid lingering in ambivalence?

DAY 24

PROVERBS 24

Wise People Do Not Envy the Wicked

Have you ever seen one of those compilation videos that shows people slipping, stumbling, and falling in embarrassing ways? They're supposed to be funny, but sometimes it's hard to laugh. Because we've all been there—doing our best to stand on our own two feet but collapsing as life kicks our legs out from under us. Despite our best intentions, failure happens, and others may laugh or point fingers as we crash to the ground.

Sometimes reading Proverbs feels a bit like that. As you read Proverbs 24, look for examples of some of the missteps that can happen in life.

READ AND RESPOND

PROVERBS 24

Saying 20

1 Do not envy the wicked,
do not desire their company;
2 for their hearts plot violence,
and their lips talk about
making trouble.

Saying 21

3 By wisdom a house is built,
and through understand-
ing it is established;
4 through knowledge its rooms are filled
with rare and beautiful treasures.

Saying 22

5 The wise prevail through great power,
and those who have knowl-
edge muster their strength.
6 Surely you need guidance to wage war,
and victory is won through
many advisers.

Saying 23

7 Wisdom is too high for fools;
in the assembly at the gate they
must not open their mouths.

Saying 24

8 Whoever plots evil
will be known as a schemer.
9 The schemes of folly are sin,
and people detest a mocker.

Saying 25

10 If you falter in a time of trouble,
how small is your strength!
11 Rescue those being led away to death;
hold back those stagger-
ing toward slaughter.
12 If you say, "But we knew
nothing about this,"
does not he who weighs
the heart perceive it?
Does not he who guards
your life know it?
Will he not repay everyone ac-
cording to what they have done?

Saying 26

13 Eat honey, my son, for it is good;
honey from the comb is
sweet to your taste.
14 Know also that wisdom
is like honey for you:
If you find it, there is a fu-
ture hope for you,
and your hope will not be cut off.

Saying 27

15 Do not lurk like a thief near
the house of the righteous,
do not plunder their dwelling place;
16 for though the righteous fall
seven times, they rise again,
but the wicked stumble
when calamity strikes.

Saying 28

17 Do not gloat when your enemy falls;
when they stumble, do not
let your heart rejoice,
18 or the LORD will see and disapprove
and turn his wrath away from them.

Saying 29

19 Do not fret because of evildoers
or be envious of the wicked,
20 for the evildoer has no future hope,
and the lamp of the
wicked will be snuffed out.

Saying 30

21 Fear the LORD and the king, my son,
and do not join with re-
bellious officials,
22 for those two will send sud-
den destruction on them,
and who knows what ca-
lamities they can bring?

FURTHER SAYINGS OF THE WISE

23 These also are sayings of the wise:

To show partiality in judging is not good:
24 Whoever says to the guilty,
"You are innocent,"
will be cursed by peoples and
denounced by nations.
25 But it will go well with those
who convict the guilty,
and rich blessing will come on them.

26 An honest answer
is like a kiss on the lips.

27 Put your outdoor work in order
and get your fields ready;
after that, build your house.

28 Do not testify against your
neighbor without cause—
would you use your lips to mislead?
29 Do not say, "I'll do to them
as they have done to me;
I'll pay them back for what they did."

30 I went past the field of a sluggard,
past the vineyard of some-
one who has no sense;
31 thorns had come up everywhere,
the ground was covered with weeds,
and the stone wall was in ruins.
32 I applied my heart to what I observed
and learned a lesson from what I saw:
33 A little sleep, a little slumber,
a little folding of the hands to rest—
34 and poverty will come
on you like a thief
and scarcity like an armed man.

It's usually the *"wicked"* who don't have sure footing—which makes it surprising to read in today's chapter that though *"the righteous fall seven times, they rise again"* (Proverbs 24:16).

Scholars note that *"seven times"* in this verse is not a precise mathematical total so much as a figure of speech meaning "a lot." The word *falls* is also broadly defined and could refer to sin, suffering, or anything else that knocks us down. But isn't the path of righteousness supposed to be smooth and straight? Why walk with God if we're going to end up on the ground so much?

Because **we will rise again.**

Look up and read Psalm 37:23–24. What do these verses say will never happen to the righteous person?

How have you experienced this as you've followed God or witnessed it in other believers' lives?

This may also remind us of the apostle Paul's later words to the church he planted in Corinth. **Look up 2 Corinthians 4:8–9 (ESV)** and write down these words below. Paul was:

"Afflicted in every way, but not ______________________."

"Perplexed, but not ______________________ to ______________________."

"Persecuted, but not ______________________."

"Struck down, but not ______________________."

Why? Because even when he fell, he fell at the foot of Jesus' cross, which is a place of victory and not defeat. And we can do the same.

Still, sometimes it's hard to stand back up. Not only do we feel unable to recover, but maybe we don't even want to—we're ashamed of how our knees buckled under the weight of temptation, or we're bruised from a painful collision with hardships we never saw coming. Frankly, *"a little sleep, a little slumber, a little folding of the hands to rest"* (Proverbs 24:33) sounds pretty good compared to walking with God, knowing there may be six more falls ahead.

But, friend, giving up is not the answer—because while our present reality is fallen, our future is redeemed.

What does Proverbs 24:14 say about hope in the Lord?

How does this encourage you to persevere, especially compared to the future of the wicked in verse 20?

Our hope in God and our awareness of our own weaknesses also help us respond compassionately when others stumble—especially those whom we would consider our enemy, or at least those who are against us. Proverbs 24:29 reminds us that as people who know what it's like to fall, we choose not to push others down but instead extend grace.

What does Proverbs 24:17–18 say we should not do when our adversaries stumble?

Consider how your own stumbling has deepened your compassion for those who trip over similar sins or endure similar pain. How might God use these parts of your story to show His love to those in need of restoration, as Proverbs 24:11 describes?

DAY 25

PROVERBS 25

Wisdom Is Knowing What Is Called for in Each Situation

Pop quiz! Do you remember the definition of *simile* from high school English class?

If not, no worries—this is the kind of quiz where you can phone a friend. A simile describes one thing by figuratively comparing it to something else using the words *like* or *as*. For example: *"Like cold water to a thirsty soul, so is good news from a far country"* (Proverbs 25:25 ESV). This gives us a more vivid, memorable image than simply saying "good news is refreshing"—which is why today's proverbs include nearly a dozen similes revealing memorable guidance for various situations.

READ AND RESPOND

PROVERBS 25

1 These are more proverbs of
Solomon, compiled by the men
of Hezekiah king of Judah:

2 It is the glory of God to
conceal a matter;
to search out a matter is
the glory of kings.
3 As the heavens are high
and the earth is deep,
so the hearts of kings are unsearchable.

4 Remove the dross from the silver,
and a silversmith can produce a vessel;
5 remove wicked officials
from the king's presence,
and his throne will be established
through righteousness.

6 Do not exalt yourself in
the king's presence,
and do not claim a place
among his great men;
7 it is better for him to say to
you, "Come up here,"
than for him to humiliate
you before his nobles.
What you have seen with your eyes

[8] do not bring hastily to court,
for what will you do in the end
if your neighbor puts you to shame?

[9] If you take your neighbor to court,
do not betray another's confidence,
[10] or the one who hears it may shame you
and the charge against you will stand.

[11] Like apples of gold in settings of silver
is a ruling rightly given.
[12] Like an earring of gold or
an ornament of fine gold
is the rebuke of a wise
judge to a listening ear.

[13] Like a snow-cooled drink
at harvest time
is a trustworthy messenger
to the one who sends him;
he refreshes the spirit of his master.
[14] Like clouds and wind without rain
is one who boasts of gifts never given.

[15] Through patience a ruler
can be persuaded,
and a gentle tongue can break a bone.

[16] If you find honey, eat just enough—
too much of it, and you will vomit.
[17] Seldom set foot in your
neighbor's house—
too much of you, and
they will hate you.

[18] Like a club or a sword or a sharp arrow
is one who gives false testimony
against a neighbor.
[19] Like a broken tooth or a lame foot
is reliance on the unfaithful
in a time of trouble.
[20] Like one who takes away a
garment on a cold day,
or like vinegar poured on a wound,
is one who sings songs to a heavy heart.

[21] If your enemy is hungry,
give him food to eat;
if he is thirsty, give him water to drink.
[22] In doing this, you will heap
burning coals on his head,
and the LORD will reward you.

[23] Like a north wind that
brings unexpected rain
is a sly tongue—which
provokes a horrified look.

[24] Better to live on a corner of the roof
than share a house with
a quarrelsome wife.
[25] Like cold water to a weary soul

is good news from a distant land.
[26] Like a muddied spring
or a polluted well
are the righteous who give
way to the wicked.

[27] It is not good to eat too much honey,
nor is it honorable to search
out matters that are too deep.

[28] Like a city whose walls
are broken through
is a person who lacks self-control.

Let's look at some examples:

VERSE	ITEM A		ITEM B	MEANING
11	Rule rightly given		Apples of gold in settings of silver	Timely, wise words are very valuable.
12				
14		IS LIKE		
18				
20				

Sometimes two verses work together to help us understand them, like how verse 11's *"ruling rightly given"* connects to verse 12's *"wise judge to a listening ear,"* both of which are compared to fine gold. This reminds us that good speakers pay attention to their listeners: Instead of speaking impulsively, they wait to talk until the other person is ready and willing to hear. This also gives the speaker time to craft a **wise** reproof—as opposed to a hasty criticism or half-baked opinion.

> Think of a situation in which you spoke too quickly or said the right thing but at the wrong time. What was the result?

> How might the idea of a *"word fitly spoken"* also relate to Proverbs 25:20?

Choosing our words well means being aware of every situation God places us in so we can speak accordingly. With those who are rejoicing, we rejoice! With those who are weeping, we weep (Romans 12:15). Happy songs would be uncalled-for in conversation with a suffering friend—and in fact, it is wise to avoid even what might *sound like* singsong to grief-stricken ears.

Bible teacher Nancy Guthrie suggests this may include platitudes like "I know just how you feel" or "At least you still have . . ." Even with good intentions, words that seem shallow or untimely in the depth of someone's pain can become *"like vinegar poured on a wound"* (Proverbs 25:20), likely eliciting an extreme or explosive reaction.

Guthrie elaborates that "what we're saying might actually be a good perspective, and it might be true, but the question is: is it helpful in this moment?"[1] This question can guide our decisions in many situations.

> For instance, justice is a godly pursuit, but what does Proverbs 25:7b–8 advise about *"hastily"* accusing others? Is a public dispute helpful in *every moment* when we think we've seen someone do wrong?

Spending time with friends is a great blessing from the Lord, but according to verse 17, is it helpful to visit friends in *every moment*? Why or why not?

While the authorship of the book of Ecclesiastes has been debated among scholars, its wisdom writings, like those we find in Proverbs, are traditionally attributed to King Solomon (Ecclesiastes 1:1). Similar to Proverbs 25, Ecclesiastes 3:1 testifies, *"There is a time for everything, and a season for every activity under the heavens."* Wisdom is the art of timeliness in our words, decisions, and relationships, according to God's will and for His glory.

One last question for today: If *"reliance on the unfaithful in a time of trouble"* is *"like a broken tooth or a lame foot"* (Proverbs 25:19), what is it "like" to trust in our faithful God? Write your own simile below:

____ is like trusting in our faithful God.

WHAT'S THE HURRY?

Does it ever feel like your world spins to the rhythm of rush?

Do you find yourself speeding—in your car or in your conversations, in your work or even in your play because just beyond this moment is another thing you need to do?

Do you feel irritable when you choose the slowest checkout line at the grocery store or angry when you get stuck in the turtle-crawl lane of traffic?

Does your to-do list run on repeat in your head all day as you push down that creeping sense of anxiety that you're forgetting something or that there's not enough time to get it all done?

Believe it or not, there's a label for this frenzied behavior pattern many of us have adopted. It's called "hurry sickness."[1]

But of course, long before our modern world coined this phrase, Solomon addressed the danger of hurry in his book of wisdom. Proverbs 19:2 says, *"Desire without knowledge is not good, how much more will hasty feet miss the way!"*

The book of Proverbs consistently discourages us from living in a perpetual rush, whether being quick to anger or just being in a hurry:

- Being *"quick-tempered"* impairs understanding and incites foolish anger (Proverbs 14:29).
- Being hot-tempered stirs up conflict (Proverbs 15:18).
- Haste leads to impulsive, costly decisions (Proverbs 21:5).
- Rushing after riches creates unstable finances (Proverbs 28:20; Proverbs 28:22).
- Speaking too quickly prompts foolish speech (Proverbs 29:20).

While Proverbs maintains that faster isn't always better, perhaps the most disturbing description of hurry was penned by Solomon's father, King David, in Psalm 39:6a: *"We are merely moving shadows, and all our busy rushing ends in nothing"* (NLT).

Haste may fill a calendar, but it can empty a soul. As Ann Voskamp writes in her book *One Thousand Gifts*, "The busyness of your life [can leave] little room for the source of your life."[2] That's why Proverbs 4:23 urges, *"Guard your heart, for everything you do flows from it."* God prizes intimacy over industry. He wants the affection of our hearts more than the accomplishment of our hands.

So what can we do to combat the hurry?

We can pray Psalm 90:12: *"Teach us to number our days, that we may gain a heart of wisdom."* This simple plea reminds us we're created for more than just counting our days. We're created to make our days count.

Let's begin conferring with God before we consult our calendar. After all, God alone knows the best rhythm for our lives. He knows how to direct our time without draining our souls. He knows how to establish our pace without hurting our hearts.

If we want to guard our hearts, we have to slow down long enough to seek God's vision as we set our schedules. Then we can be quick to listen when He speaks to our souls.

10 WAYS TO SLOW DOWN

1. Unplug for a set amount of time each day.
2. Wherever you are, be all there.
3. Look up—at the sky, the clouds, the leaves on the trees, the stars at night—and breathe deeply. Or connect with nature in your own favorite way.
4. Say "no" to something that drains your soul so you can say "yes" to something that fills it.
5. Take a prayer walk.
6. Keep a gratitude journal.
7. Take time to taste your food.
8. Begin each day in God's Word. (If we want to keep in step with the Spirit throughout our day [Galatians 5:25], it helps to calibrate our steps from the start.)
9. Send a handwritten letter instead of a text.
10. Listen without thinking about what you're going to say next.

DAY 26

PROVERBS 26

Trusting the Wise Is Wise; Trusting the Foolish Is Foolish

The definition of *trust* is "to believe that someone is good and honest and will not harm you, or that something is safe and reliable."[1] With this in mind, it makes perfect sense that Scripture tells us to *"trust in the LORD with all [our] heart"* (Proverbs 3:5). God is completely good, honest, safe, and reliable!

However, Proverbs 26 reminds us that when it comes to other people—everyone besides Jesus—trusting wisely requires acknowledging the limits and weaknesses we all have as humans. That doesn't mean we lean into cynicism; instead, we lean into wisdom, relying on the Holy Spirit to develop trustworthiness in us and teach us to recognize it in others.

> What traits, habits, attitudes, or behaviors would you say are characteristic of trustworthy people?

READ AND RESPOND

PROVERBS 26

1 Like snow in summer or rain in harvest,
honor is not fitting for a fool.
2 Like a fluttering sparrow
or a darting swallow,
an undeserved curse does
not come to rest.
3 A whip for the horse, a
bridle for the donkey,
and a rod for the backs of fools!
4 Do not answer a fool
according to his folly,
or you yourself will be just like him.
5 Answer a fool according to his folly,
or he will be wise in his own eyes.

6 Sending a message by the hands of a fool
is like cutting off one's feet
or drinking poison.
7 Like the useless legs of one who is lame
is a proverb in the mouth of a fool.
8 Like tying a stone in a sling
is the giving of honor to a fool.
9 Like a thornbush in a drunkard's hand
is a proverb in the mouth of a fool.
10 Like an archer who wounds at random
is one who hires a fool or any passer-by.
11 As a dog returns to its vomit,
so fools repeat their folly.
12 Do you see a person wise
in their own eyes?
There is more hope for
a fool than for them.

13 A sluggard says, "There's
a lion in the road,
a fierce lion roaming the streets!"
14 As a door turns on its hinges,
so a sluggard turns on his bed.
15 A sluggard buries his hand in the dish;
he is too lazy to bring it
back to his mouth.
16 A sluggard is wiser in his own eyes
than seven people who
answer discreetly.

17 Like one who grabs a
stray dog by the ears
is someone who rushes into
a quarrel not their own.

18 Like a maniac shooting
flaming arrows of death
19 is one who deceives their neighbor
and says, "I was only joking!"

20 Without wood a fire goes out;
without a gossip a quarrel dies down.
21 As charcoal to embers
and as wood to fire,
so is a quarrelsome person
for kindling strife.
22 The words of a gossip are
like choice morsels;
they go down to the inmost parts.

23 Like a coating of silver
dross on earthenware
are fervent lips with an evil heart.
24 Enemies disguise themselves
with their lips,
but in their hearts they harbor deceit.
25 Though their speech is
charming, do not believe them,
for seven abominations fill their hearts.
26 Their malice may be
concealed by deception,
but their wickedness will be

exposed in the assembly.
27 Whoever digs a pit will fall into it;
if someone rolls a stone, it
will roll back on them.
28 A lying tongue hates those it hurts,
and a flattering mouth works ruin.

Let's see how Proverbs 26 helps us build a profile of trustworthiness.

1. A trustworthy person is honest. Verses 18–19 warn us *not* to trust *"one who deceives their neighbor and says, 'I was only joking!'"* While this may seem like a minor deception, it reminds us that a trustworthy person is consistently honest and doesn't make excuses or exceptions even for "white lies." Proverbs 26:18 compares deceptive words to *"flaming arrows of death."*

Look up and read James 3:5.

What does this verse also say about the tongue?

How does this motivate us to speak honestly?

2. A trustworthy person is honorable. Proverbs 26:1 says a dishonorable or foolish person is *"like snow in summer or rain in harvest,"* an image that would have been deeply unnerving for the original readers of Proverbs. In ancient Israel, snow in summer was more than just unseasonal—it was disastrous, destroying crops and leaving people hungry.[2]

In contrast, look up the following proverbs and describe what honorable character looks like:

- Proverbs 11:16:

- Proverbs 29:23:

- Proverbs 20:3:

3. A trustworthy person learns from their mistakes. Proverbs 26:11 says, *"As a dog returns to its vomit, so fools repeat their folly."* Yep, that's an image you really can't unsee. And this is the point: When we view our foolishness in the light of God's Truth, we see clearly that we don't have to—or *want* to—keep making the same errors.

In King Solomon's time, a "fool" was generally a person opposed to God's wisdom, His commands, His covenant, and His people. But even as followers of God, we are to examine ourselves for folly in our own hearts. We all make unwise choices sometimes, but instead of returning to our failings, we can return to the Lord, asking Him to help us move forward.

> Is there a *"folly"* you keep returning to, repeating the same mistake or repeatedly feeling guilty? How could you break the cycle by surrendering this issue to the Lord?

4. A trustworthy person is loving but not naive. Verse 10 describes how trusting an unknown or unreliable person *"wounds everyone,"* seemingly because it involves a lack of wisdom in both the giver and the receiver of such trust. Someone who hires a *"passing fool"* (a person they don't know well or have good reason to trust) takes an unnecessary risk.

Of course, when Jesus commands us to love our neighbor (Mark 12:31), He means *everyone*—so we don't withhold Christlike love even from people who may disappoint us. But Christlike love can include setting appropriate boundaries for the good of others and ourselves.

> First Corinthians 13:6 says love *"does not delight in evil."* At the same time, love *"always trusts, always hopes, always perseveres"* (1 Corinthians 13:7). How can we hold these truths in tension as we choose who and how to trust wisely?

DAY 27

PROVERBS 27

Wisdom in Friendship Counsels & Strengthens

Earlier in this study, we talked about innate human needs for food, drink, and other essentials that make survival possible. Today's reading focuses on a provision from God that we might not think of as a survival essential, but it's life-sustaining in its own way: friendship.

Christian writer Marshall Segal observes, "The beauty and worth of God cannot be exhausted by one pair of eyes, by one finite mind and heart. Therefore, two really can see more than one. The more we share of him, the more we have of him."[1] Especially between followers of Jesus, our faith strengthens our friendships to become not only healthy but holy. That's why we can call our fellow believers *brothers and sisters* in Christ.

READ AND RESPOND

PROVERBS 27

1 Do not boast about tomorrow,
for you do not know
what a day may bring.

2 Let someone else praise you,
and not your own mouth;
an outsider, and not your own lips.

3 Stone is heavy and sand a burden,
but a fool's provocation
is heavier than both.

4 Anger is cruel and fury overwhelming,
but who can stand before jealousy?

5 Better is open rebuke
than hidden love.

6 Wounds from a friend can be trusted,
but an enemy multiplies kisses.

7 One who is full loathes
honey from the comb,
but to the hungry even what
is bitter tastes sweet.

8 Like a bird that flees its nest
is anyone who flees from home.

9 Perfume and incense bring
joy to the heart,
and the pleasantness of a friend
springs from their heartfelt advice.

10 Do not forsake your friend
or a friend of your family,
and do not go to your relative's
house when disaster strikes you—
better a neighbor nearby
than a relative far away.

11 Be wise, my son, and
bring joy to my heart;
then I can answer anyone who
treats me with contempt.

12 The prudent see danger
and take refuge,
but the simple keep going
and pay the penalty.

13 Take the garment of one who
puts up security for a stranger;
hold it in pledge if it is
done for an outsider.

14 If anyone loudly blesses their
neighbor early in the morning,
it will be taken as a curse.

15 A quarrelsome wife is like the dripping
of a leaky roof in a rainstorm;
16 restraining her is like
restraining the wind
or grasping oil with the hand.

17 As iron sharpens iron,
so one person sharpens another.

18 The one who guards a fig
tree will eat its fruit,
and whoever protects their
master will be honored.

19 As water reflects the face,
so one's life reflects the heart.

20 Death and Destruction
are never satisfied,
and neither are human eyes.

21 The crucible for silver and
the furnace for gold,
but people are tested by their praise.

22 Though you grind a fool in a mortar,
grinding them like grain with a pestle,
you will not remove their

folly from them.
23 Be sure you know the
condition of your flocks,
give careful attention to your herds;
24 for riches do not endure forever,
and a crown is not secure
for all generations.
25 When the hay is removed
and new growth appears
and the grass from the
hills is gathered in,
26 the lambs will provide
you with clothing,
and the goats with the price of a field.
27 You will have plenty of goats'
milk to feed your family
and to nourish your female servants.

What do Proverbs 27:9 and verse 17 suggest about the blessings of godly friendship?

How do these verses compare or contrast to some of the friendships in your life?

Together, these two verses offer an interesting double image of friendship as both sweet and sharpening: At times, heartfelt advice and support from friends covers us like a beautiful fragrance (v. 9), and at other times, righteous friends challenge and convict us in ways that may feel like the iron being sharpened (v. 17). God uses *both* of these things—encouragement and accountability—to build our character for our good and His glory.

What would it be like to have a friend who's always sharpening you but never sweet?

What would it be like to have a friend who's always sweet but never offers sharpening?

Next, let's look at verse 14. A plain reading of this verse addresses social skills and courtesy, an important part of any relationship. It's possible to be well-meaning but obnoxious early in the morning, which we'd want to avoid. But verse 14 may also elaborate on the distinction between friendship and flattery: *"If anyone loudly blesses their neighbor early in the morning,"* they could be covering up ulterior motives that are anything but friendly. David Guzik suggests that "the sense here is of an over-the-top greeting and blessing, meant to flatter and manipulate . . . something is amiss in such excessive praise."[2]

A "loud" blessing (v. 14) may likewise imply shouting from afar; however, a true friend draws near in the day-to-day. How could we smell sweet perfume from a distance (v. 9)? How could iron sharpen iron without getting close enough to touch (v. 17)?

Proverbs 27:10b says, *"Better a neighbor nearby than a relative far away."* Today, we can have friends on social media whom we may not ever meet in person, yet Proverbs 27 reminds us that a nearby neighbor is often more helpful (in an emergency, for example) than a family member at a distance. Modern technology is a blessing that helps us stay in touch with friends all over the map, but let's also remember to invest in relationships with our nearby neighbors, friends, and local church members.

The Message paraphrase of John 1:14 says Jesus showed His love for us when He *"became flesh and blood, and moved into the neighborhood."* While sitting around a table and sharing a meal with them in person, what did Jesus call His disciples in John 15:15?

Think of at least one godly person in your life whom you'd like to build a stronger friendship with (or ask God to show you a potential friend He has placed in proximity to you). How could you strengthen that friendship this week?

EXAMPLES OF FAITHFUL FRIENDSHIP IN SCRIPTURE

MOSES AND AARON	These two men were brothers, and we might also consider them friends. God used Aaron's speaking skills to help Moses communicate His words to the nation of Israel. Aaron also famously strengthened and supported Moses during a battle against Israel's enemy Amalek.	*"The LORD . . . said, 'What about your brother, Aaron the Levite? I know he can speak well. He is already on his way to meet you, and he will be glad to see you. You shall speak to him and put words in his mouth; I will help both of you speak and will teach you what to do"* (Exodus 4:14–15). *"As long as Moses held up his hands, the Israelites were winning . . . . When Moses' hands grew tired, they took a stone and put it under him and he sat on it. Aaron and Hur held his hands up—one on one side, one on the other—so that his hands remained steady . . ."* (Exodus 17:11–12).

DAVID AND JONATHAN	Jonathan was the son of David's enemy, King Saul, but Jonathan and David were best friends, and their relationship was characterized by mutually sharing burdens and protecting each other.	*"Jonathan became one in spirit with David, and he loved him as himself"* (1 Samuel 18:1). "Only Jonathan and David knew" (1 Samuel 20:39b).
JESUS AND HIS DISCIPLES	Jesus had many followers during His life on earth, but He had 12 close friends: men He spent most of His time doing ministry with. He taught them, ate with them, traveled with them, listened to them, and served them. Even those who betrayed Him, He was willing to forgive.	*"I no longer call you servants, because a servant does not know his master's business. Instead, I have called you friends, for everything that I learned from my Father I have made known to you"* (John 15:15). *"One of them, the disciple whom Jesus loved, was reclining next to him"* (John 13:23). *"When they had finished eating, Jesus said to Simon Peter, 'Simon, son of John, do you love me more than these?' He said to him, 'Yes, Lord; you know that I love you'"* (John 21:15).

PAUL AND MINISTRY PARTNERS	Gospel friendships were essential to the apostle Paul's ministry: Paul's friends prayed for him, suffered with him, and comforted him, and he did the same for them. Paul wrote letters to his friends when they were apart but celebrated quality time together.	*"Aristarchus my fellow prisoner greets you, and Mark the cousin of Barnabas (concerning whom you have received instructions—if he comes to you, welcome him), and Jesus who is called Justus . . . they have been a comfort to me"* (Colossians 4:10–11 ESV). *"I remember you [Timothy] constantly in my prayers night and day. As I remember your tears, I long to see you, that I may be filled with joy. I am reminded of your sincere faith . . ."* (2 Timothy 1:3–5 ESV).
JOHN AND FRIENDS IN THE CHURCH	The apostle John spoke of friends he desired to see face to face, friends who were both near and far, and each of their names was important to him.	*"I had much to write to you, but I would rather not write with pen and ink. I hope to see you soon, and we will talk face to face. Peace be to you. The friends greet you. Greet the friends, each by name"* (3 John 1:13–15 ESV).

PROVERBS 28

Wise Decisions & God's Law Go Hand in Hand

Today there are many popular TV shows, podcasts, movies, and novels featuring a "criminal mastermind" as the main character. The brilliant burglar who plans an untraceable heist, the conspirator who escapes an inescapable prison, the vigilante who avoids capture through evasive hijinks . . .

Sound familiar? While our world may encourage us to be entertained or even impressed by "getting away with" wrongdoing, Proverbs 28 reminds us that our response to evil reveals where our loyalties truly lie. As you read, notice how Solomon contrasts those who abandon God's instruction with those who actively resist wrongdoing—and how true understanding of justice begins with seeking the Lord.

READ AND RESPOND

PROVERBS 28

1 The wicked flee though no one pursues,
but the righteous are as bold as a lion.

2 When a country is rebel-
lious, it has many rulers,
but a ruler with discernment and
knowledge maintains order.

3 A ruler who oppresses the poor
is like a driving rain that
leaves no crops.

4 Those who forsake instruc-
tion praise the wicked,
but those who heed it resist them.

5 Evildoers do not under-
stand what is right,
but those who seek the
LORD understand it fully.

6 Better the poor whose walk is blameless
than the rich whose ways are perverse.

[7] A discerning son heeds instruction,
but a companion of glut-
tons disgraces his father.

[8] Whoever increases wealth by tak-
ing interest or profit from the poor
amasses it for another, who
will be kind to the poor.

[9] If anyone turns a deaf ear
to my instruction,
even their prayers are detestable.

[10] Whoever leads the up-
right along an evil path
will fall into their own trap,
but the blameless will re-
ceive a good inheritance.

[11] The rich are wise in their own eyes;
one who is poor and discern-
ing sees how deluded they are.

[12] When the righteous tri-
umph, there is great elation;
but when the wicked rise to
power, people go into hiding.

[13] Whoever conceals their
sins does not prosper,
but the one who confesses and
renounces them finds mercy.

[14] Blessed is the one who always trem-
bles before God, but whoever hard-
ens their heart falls into trouble.

[15] Like a roaring lion or a charging bear
is a wicked ruler over a helpless people.

[16] A tyrannical ruler practices extortion,
but one who hates ill-gotten
gain will enjoy a long reign.

[17] Anyone tormented by
the guilt of murder
will seek refuge in the grave;
let no one hold them back.

[18] The one whose walk is
blameless is kept safe,
but the one whose ways are per-
verse will fall into the pit.

[19] Those who work their land
will have abundant food,
but those who chase fantasies
will have their fill of poverty.

[20] A faithful person will be richly blessed,
but one eager to get rich
will not go unpunished.

21 To show partiality is not good—
yet a person will do wrong
for a piece of bread.

22 The stingy are eager to get rich
and are unaware that pov-
erty awaits them.

23 Whoever rebukes a person
will in the end gain favor
rather than one who has
a flattering tongue.

24 Whoever robs their father or mother
and says, "It's not wrong,"
is partner to one who destroys.

25 The greedy stir up conflict,
but those who trust in the
LORD will prosper.

26 Those who trust in them-
selves are fools,
but those who walk in wis-
dom are kept safe.

27 Those who give to the
poor will lack nothing,
but those who close their eyes
to them receive many curses.

28 When the wicked rise to
power, people go into hiding;
but when the wicked
perish, the righteous thrive.

Throughout today's reading, *"the law,"* or *torah* in Hebrew, refers to the rules for righteous living that God gave His people in the Old Testament. For quick reference, we can look to the Ten Commandments as an overarching summary. Write down as many commandments as you can from memory, and then read Exodus 20 for the rest.

When Proverbs 28:7 declares that *"a discerning son heeds instruction,"* the Ten Commandments is the law it's referring to, connecting godly obedience and justice to wisdom.

Meanwhile, breaking God's laws is connected to ignorance: *"Evildoers do not understand what is right"* (Proverbs 28:5).

We also see that while wisdom leads to thoughtful decision-making based on God's Truth, disobedience dulls and distorts our minds such that *"a person will do wrong for a piece of bread"* (v. 21).

This may seem like a ridiculous exaggeration—seriously, a piece of bread? **But let's read Genesis 25:29–34.** How and why did Esau decide to give his birthright to his brother, Jacob?

Next, read Genesis 3:1–13. What law did God give Adam and Eve? How and why did they break it?

Of course, the problem here isn't the food. The problem is that sin fools us into believing the only things that matter in life are earthly things we can sink our teeth into *right now*—wealth, fame, pleasure, comfort, power—so we're willing to do anything for just one bite.

But God's law gives us an eternal perspective. Though sinners scheme and plot, the only real Mastermind in the universe is the One who created it, and He upholds justice for the good of those who love Him. For instance, Proverbs 28:8 assures that extortionists and embezzlers who line their pockets with stolen cash will someday be humiliated to realize that, all along, they were really making deposits into God's heavenly account, and He will use it to provide for the poor. In the end, no one actually "gets away with" evil. In fact, what the wicked mean for evil, God will redeem and use for good (Genesis 50:20; Romans 8:28).

The cross is the ultimate example of this! *"None of the rulers of this age understood it, for if they had, they would not have crucified the Lord of glory. However, as it is written, 'What no eye has seen, what no ear has heard, and what no human mind has conceived'—the things God has prepared for those who love him"* (1 Corinthians 2:8–9).

To wrap up, let's go back through this chapter and list all the verbs associated with both following God's law and denying it. Include the verse number as you go:

VERSE	THOSE WHO DENY GOD'S LAW	THOSE WHO FOLLOW GOD'S LAW
Examples v. 1	Flee	Are as bold as a lion
v. 2	Have many rulers	Maintain order
v. 4	Forsake instruction	Heed instruction and resist wickedness

How does this list help you to see how following God's law helps you not only make better decisions but benefit from them as well?

DAY 29

PROVERBS 29

Wise Leadership Is Godly Leadership

Did you ever play "Follow the Leader" as a kid? Here are the rules if you need a refresher: Whatever the designated leader does (stomping, clapping, jumping, etc.) everyone else has to do it too.

That's it. As you might imagine, the game usually lasts about 10 minutes—because the followers get tired of obeying arbitrary commands. And in this case, what's true on the playground is true in life: Today's proverbs reveal that a wise leader is not just someone who makes people listen to them but someone who's worth listening to.

READ AND RESPOND

PROVERBS 29

1 Whoever remains stiff-
necked after many rebukes
will suddenly be de-
stroyed—without remedy.

2 When the righteous thrive,
the people rejoice;
when the wicked rule,
the people groan.

3 A man who loves wisdom
brings joy to his father,
but a companion of prosti-
tutes squanders his wealth.

4 By justice a king gives a country stability,
but those who are greedy
for bribes tear it down.

5 Those who flatter their neighbors
are spreading nets for their feet.

6 Evildoers are snared by their own sin,
but the righteous shout
for joy and are glad.

7 The righteous care about
justice for the poor,
but the wicked have no such concern.

8 Mockers stir up a city,
but the wise turn away anger.

9 If a wise person goes to
court with a fool,
the fool rages and scoffs,
and there is no peace.

10 The bloodthirsty hate a
person of integrity
and seek to kill the upright.

11 Fools give full vent to their rage,
but the wise bring calm in the end.

12 If a ruler listens to lies,
all his officials become wicked.

13 The poor and the oppres-
sor have this in common:
The LORD gives sight
to the eyes of both.

14 If a king judges the poor with fairness,
his throne will be established forever.

15 A rod and a reprimand impart wisdom,
but a child left undisci-
plined disgraces its mother.

16 When the wicked thrive, so does sin,
but the righteous will
see their downfall.

17 Discipline your children, and
they will give you peace;
they will bring you the de-
lights you desire.

18 Where there is no revelation,
people cast off restraint;
but blessed is the one who
heeds wisdom's instruction.

19 Servants cannot be cor-
rected by mere words;
though they understand,
they will not respond.

20 Do you see someone
who speaks in haste?
There is more hope for
a fool than for them.

21 A servant pampered from youth
will turn out to be insolent.

22 An angry person stirs up conflict,
and a hot-tempered per-
son commits many sins.

23 Pride brings a person low,

but the lowly in spirit gain honor.

24 The accomplices of thieves
are their own enemies;
they are put under oath
and dare not testify.

25 Fear of man will prove to be a snare,
but whoever trusts in the
Lord is kept safe.

26 Many seek an audience with a ruler,
but it is from the Lord
that one gets justice.

27 The righteous detest the dishonest;
the wicked detest the upright.

Some of us have professional or official leadership titles, but God has given all of us authority and influence in different ways. Below, list a few areas of your life in which you guide, teach, assist, oversee, or set an example for others:

Proverbs 29:2 teaches that *"when the righteous thrive"* in power and influence, *"the people rejoice."* Everyone knows their concerns will be considered and their dignity will be honored by a godly leader—because that's how God Himself leads us. While worldly authorities are easily bribed and partial to prestige (v. 4), verse 7 says *"the righteous care about justice for the poor."* The Hebrew word for *"knows"* **יָדַע** (*yada*) in this verse implies concern, care, and close attention to the least powerful people in the room.[1]

Looking at the roles you listed above, how can you intentionally care for people in your areas of influence who may feel unheard or unseen?

Christian writer Lore Ferguson Wilbert puts it this way: "The crowning achievement of every kingdom leader is to be the least, the last, and the lowest . . . . It may not look like the glamorous service you suspect."[2]

Sometimes it looks like persevering through hard conversations.
Sometimes it looks like helping a co-worker redo a task without criticizing their mistakes.
Sometimes it looks like driving an extra hour each week to disciple a new believer from church.

What examples of unglamorous leadership have you seen in your home, church, or community?

Is there any "glamour" you could set aside to be a more Christlike leader?

While several of today's Scriptures offer guidance for kings and rulers (vv. 4, 14, 26), for most of us, negotiating dinner with our kids is enough domestic policy for a lifetime. Thankfully, scholars note that Proverbs 29 includes both "ruling" and "rearing" Scriptures to help us become God-glorifying leaders within our families.

Read the following verses and fill in the chart.

	WHAT IS THE RESULT OF DISCIPLINE?
PROVERBS 29:15	
PROVERBS 29:17	

Based on verse 22, how do we know that the discipline described in verses 15 and 17 is **not** motivated by anger?

How would you define godly discipline apart from penal discipline?

What do you think godly discipline is actually motivated by?

Of all the ways God could reveal Himself to us, He has chosen to identify Himself as both our King and our Father—and in this sense, the ways we lead and submit to earthly leaders reflect how we relate to God. If our child disobeys, it's good to respond with appropriate consequences, but we also remember that *"as a father has compassion on his children, so the LORD has compassion on those who fear him"* (Psalm 103:13). If someone undermines our authority at work, we can remember that all authority ultimately belongs to God: *"It is from the LORD that one gets justice"* (Proverbs 29:26).

How might this perspective change the choices you make as you lead (and follow leaders) in your daily life circumstances?

DAY 30

PROVERBS 30

Only God Knows Everything

Having meticulously examined wisdom from all angles—financial, social, familial, moral, professional, spiritual, and more—over the course of 29 chapters, we might expect some confidence from the sage scribe here at the end of Proverbs. But if so, chapter 30's first verses might come as a shock.

READ AND RESPOND

PROVERBS 30

1 The sayings of Agur son of
Jakeh—an inspired utterance.

This man's utterance to Ithiel:

"I am weary, God,
but I can prevail.
2 Surely I am only a brute, not a man;
I do not have human understanding.
3 I have not learned wisdom,
nor have I attained to the
knowledge of the Holy One.
4 Who has gone up to heaven
and come down?
Whose hands have
gathered up the wind?
Who has wrapped up the
waters in a cloak?
Who has established all
the ends of the earth?
What is his name, and what
is the name of his son?
Surely you know!

5 "Every word of God is flawless;
he is a shield to those who
take refuge in him.
6 Do not add to his words,
or he will rebuke you
and prove you a liar.

7 "Two things I ask of you, LORD;
do not refuse me before I die:
8 Keep falsehood and lies far from me;
give me neither poverty nor riches,
but give me only my daily bread.

[9] Otherwise, I may have too
much and disown you
and say, 'Who is the LORD?'
Or I may become poor and steal,
and so dishonor the name of my God.

[10] "Do not slander a servant
to their master,
or they will curse you, and
you will pay for it.

[11] "There are those who curse their fathers
and do not bless their mothers;
[12] those who are pure in their own eyes
and yet are not cleansed of their filth;
[13] those whose eyes are ever so haughty,
whose glances are so disdainful;
[14] those whose teeth are swords
and whose jaws are set with knives
to devour the poor from the earth
and the needy from among mankind.

[15] "The leech has two daughters.
'Give! Give!' they cry.

"There are three things that
are never satisfied,
four that never say, 'Enough!':
[16] the grave, the barren womb,
land, which is never
satisfied with water,
and fire, which never says, 'Enough!'

[17] "The eye that mocks a father,
that scorns an aged mother,
will be pecked out by the
ravens of the valley,
will be eaten by the vultures.

[18] "There are three things that
are too amazing for me,
four that I do not understand:
[19] the way of an eagle in the sky,
the way of a snake on a rock,
the way of a ship on the high seas,
and the way of a man
with a young woman.

[20] "This is the way of an
adulterous woman:
She eats and wipes her mouth
and says, 'I've done nothing wrong.'

[21] "Under three things the earth trembles,
under four it cannot bear up:
[22] a servant who becomes king,
a godless fool who gets plenty to eat,
[23] a contemptible woman
who gets married,
and a servant who
displaces her mistress.

24 "Four things on earth are small,
yet they are extremely wise:
25 Ants are creatures of little strength,
yet they store up their
food in the summer;
26 hyraxes are creatures of little power,
yet they make their home in the crags;
27 locusts have no king,
yet they advance together in ranks;
28 a lizard can be caught with the hand,
yet it is found in kings' palaces.

29 "There are three things that
are stately in their stride,
four that move with stately bearing:
30 a lion, mighty among beasts,
who retreats before nothing;
31 a strutting rooster, a he-goat,
and a king secure against revolt.

32 "If you play the fool and exalt yourself,
or if you plan evil,
clap your hand over your mouth!
33 For as churning cream produces butter,
and as twisting the nose
produces blood,
so stirring up anger produces strife."

Based on this not-exactly-glowing introduction, Agur seems an unlikely candidate for sharing any great wisdom. However, scholars note that his extreme modesty is actually the bedrock premise of his five-part argument about the divine origin of wisdom:

1. Human knowledge is limited (vv. 2–3).
2. True wisdom comes from limitless knowledge (v. 4).
3. Only God has limitless knowledge (v. 4).
4. God's people are His children (v. 4).
5. God has revealed wisdom to His children in His Word (vv. 5–6).[1]

In verse 4, Agur asks, *"What is [God's] name, and what is the name of his son?"* This might seem obvious, but let's consider: Do you know God's name?

How do you know it?

If you learned God's name from a parent or pastor, where did they learn it?

If you learned it from the Bible, how did it get there?

How did the biblical writers find out God's name?

Theologians call these *epistemological* questions, or questions about how we know what we know.

Ultimately, they lead us to realize "one can only know what is His name (God's nature, character) and His Son's name by God's own revelation."[2] There's one main question everyone must ask to live wisely—Who is God?—and only God can answer it for us. Thankfully, He has done just that! In fact, Proverbs 30:4 prophetically points to God's ultimate revelation of Himself to humankind through His Son, Jesus.

Agur's constant counting in Proverbs 30 further emphasizes humanity's limited understanding and our dependence on divine revelation. Unlike God's knowledge, ours can be quantified in terms of *"four things"* (v. 24) or *"three things"* (v. 21) because our brains can only store so much information. On top of that, there's information we can't even access because it's *"too amazing"* (v. 18). Our Creator is uncountable and infinite.

If Agur could only think of four things in the world that he didn't understand (Proverbs 30:18), he might have been tempted to take pride in his intelligence. But how do verses like these explain Agur's humility before the God of *infinite* wisdom and power?

My mouth will tell of your righteous deeds,
of your saving acts all day long—
though I know not how to relate them all (Psalm 71:15).

But if I were you, I would appeal to God;
I would lay my cause before him.
He performs wonders that cannot be fathomed,
miracles that cannot be counted (Job 5:8–9).

How does meditating on God's limitlessness humble you?

Follow Agur's example by writing four things you don't understand about the world; then thank God, the world's Creator, that He does understand them.

Proverbs 30:21–23 reminds us that choosing wisdom means choosing a life of dependence on God, not a life of promoting ourselves from ignorance to intelligence, poverty to riches, or even rejection to acceptance. After all, it's the *"things on earth [that] are small"*—and content with their smallness—that *"are extremely wise"* (v. 24).

Read Jesus' words in Matthew 6:28–30.

How do His words echo the truth of Proverbs 30:24–28?

As one commentator puts it, "Jesus embodied what Agur commends. Though he was God, he humbled himself in order to become a man." Therefore, "Agur might say that though you are a human, humble yourself so . . . you might learn wisdom and ascend to God with Christ."[3]

DAY 31

PROVERBS 31

A Wise Woman Fears the Lord

We've made it to the end of Proverbs. And in our final day together, we will read a chapter of Scripture that might feel like it was written for a different culture and sets up an unattainable standard of womanhood. Today, let's set those assumptions aside. If the book of Proverbs has taught us anything, we know that God values our heart more than our deeds. He desires obedience rather than sacrifice.

So, as you read Proverbs 31, look beyond the specific activities described and watch for the enduring principles that reveal what it means to live with wisdom, strength, and reverence for God.

READ AND RESPOND

PROVERBS 31

1 The sayings of King Lemuel—an
inspired utterance his mother taught him.

2 Listen, my son! Listen,
son of my womb!
Listen, my son, the
answer to my prayers!
3 Do not spend your strength on women,
your vigor on those who ruin kings.

4 It is not for kings, Lemuel—
it is not for kings to drink wine,
not for rulers to crave beer,
5 lest they drink and forget
what has been decreed,
and deprive all the
oppressed of their rights.
6 Let beer be for those who are perishing,
wine for those who are in anguish!
7 Let them drink and forget their poverty
and remember their misery no more.

8 Speak up for those who cannot
speak for themselves,
for the rights of all who are destitute.
9 Speak up and judge fairly;
defend the rights of the
poor and needy.

EPILOGUE: THE WIFE OF NOBLE CHARACTER

10 A wife of noble character who can find?
She is worth far more than rubies.
11 Her husband has full confidence in her
and lacks nothing of value.
12 She brings him good, not harm,
all the days of her life.
13 She selects wool and flax
and works with eager hands.
14 She is like the merchant ships,
bringing her food from afar.
15 She gets up while it is still night;
she provides food for her family
and portions for her female servants.
16 She considers a field and buys it;
out of her earnings she plants a vineyard.
17 She sets about her work vigorously;
her arms are strong for her tasks.
18 She sees that her trading is profitable,
and her lamp does not go out at night.
19 In her hand she holds the distaff
and grasps the spindle with her fingers.
20 She opens her arms to the poor
and extends her hands to the needy.
21 When it snows, she has no fear for her household;
for all of them are clothed in scarlet.
22 She makes coverings for her bed;
she is clothed in fine linen and purple.
23 Her husband is respected at the city gate,
where he takes his seat among the elders of the land.
24 She makes linen garments and sells them,
and supplies the merchants with sashes.
25 She is clothed with strength and dignity;
she can laugh at the days to come.
26 She speaks with wisdom,
and faithful instruction is on her tongue.
27 She watches over the affairs of her household
and does not eat the bread of idleness.
28 Her children arise and call her blessed;
her husband also, and he praises her:
29 "Many women do noble things,
but you surpass them all."
30 Charm is deceptive, and beauty is fleeting;
but a woman who fears the LORD is to be praised.
31 Honor her for all that her hands have done,
and let her works bring her praise at the city gate.

What a list of requirements! As we look at verse 10 of today's passage—*"A wife of noble character who can find?"*—we might think, *Great question! Who could measure up?*

But let's consider this insight from women's discipleship leader Adrien Segal: "God never urges us to feel guilty for not having gifts we've not been given, or for not doing good we're physically unable to do. So, if the Proverbs 31 woman only makes us feel guilty or inadequate, we're likely not understanding her in the way God designed."[1]

> Pause for a quick "heart check": Do you feel any guilt, jealousy, discontentment, or bitterness in response to today's passage?

> Confess those feelings to the Lord below, asking Him to help you understand His true heart for these Scriptures.

Let's first note that, like much of Proverbs, chapter 31 is not a prescriptive text. In other words, it is not a set of requirements for all women always. Just as not all are called to make and sell linen garments (v. 24), not all are called to marriage or motherhood like we see in this chapter; however, the Proverbs 31 woman demonstrates godliness in a variety of contexts and relationships, so there's applicable guidance here for all walks of life.

> Whatever your current season looks like, note one verse from Proverbs 31 that encourages you today and one verse that highlights an area where you want to grow or make better decisions.

> "My one verse":

Another important clarification is that Proverbs 31 reveals a *way of life* rather than a *day in the life* of a godly woman. God's Word celebrates the accomplishments of the Proverbs 31 woman by cataloging her many great deeds—a practice usually reserved for celebrating war heroes in ancient literature.[2] But still, the idea is not that she *"[brings] her food from afar"* (v. 14), *"considers a field and buys it . . . plants a vineyard"* (v. 16), and *"makes coverings for her bed"* (v. 22) every 24 hours. In fact, if Proverbs 31 were a daily to-do list, it would be the to-do list of a woman who had much to learn about honoring her own limitations and resting in the Lord.

If someone read your to-do list today, what might they conclude about your priorities?

How can you honor your own limitations at the same time as you honor God with your choices and plans?

After reading the Proverbs 31 woman's impressive résumé, it's easy to assume her family *"call[s] her blessed"* and *"praises her"* (v. 28) because of all her providing, bringing, delivering, working, and teaching in verses 11–27. But let's look at verse 30 to focus on the most important truth.

Why is she *"to be praised"* (v. 30)?

It's not because she works wonders with a spindle and flax.
It's not because of her successful business ventures.
It's not because she feeds her kids organic, home-cooked dinners seven nights a week.

It's because she follows God faithfully, and her identity is secure in Him.

As tempted as we may be to compare ourselves to the Proverbs 31 woman, she spends no time comparing herself to others in this famous chapter. Why do you think that is? How does reverence for our incomparable God lead us away from envious comparisons?

PROVERBS 31: EDEN REVISITED

Scholars debate whether the Proverbs 31 woman was a real person or simply an aspirational archetype, but either way, it's interesting to note that the biblical description of the *"excellent wife"* (Proverbs 31:10 ESV) is almost directly opposite to the biblical description of Eve in the garden of Eden. In this sense, the Proverbs 31 woman and Eve embody the two contrasting paths of Proverbs: sin and godliness, disobedience and obedience, foolishness and wisdom.

GENESIS 3	PROVERBS 31
Eve listened to the voice of the deceiver. *"He said to the woman, 'Did God actually say, "You shall not eat of any tree in the garden"?'"* (v. 1 ESV).	**The God-fearing woman listens to His Truth.** *"Charm is deceitful, and beauty is vain, but a woman who fears the LORD is to be praised"* (v. 30 ESV).
Eve filled her mouth with sin. *"So when the woman saw . . . the tree was to be desired to make one wise, she took of its fruit and ate . . ."* (v. 6 ESV).	**The mouth of the God-fearing woman is filled with righteousness.** *"She opens her mouth with wisdom, and the teaching of kindness is on her tongue"* (v. 26 ESV).
Eve took the forbidden fruit and brought death into the world. *"The woman said, 'The serpent deceived me, and I ate'"* (v. 13b ESV).	**The God-fearing woman cultivates fruit, bringing forth life.** *". . . with the fruit of her hands she plants a vineyard"* (v. 16 ESV).

Eve harmed her husband by offering him the forbidden fruit. *". . . she also gave some to her husband who was with her, and he ate"* (v. 6 ESV).	**The God-fearing woman does not tempt her husband with sin.** *"She does him good, and not harm, all the days of her life"* (v. 12 ESV).
Eve clothed herself because she was afraid and ashamed. *". . . they knew that they were naked. And they sewed fig leaves together and made themselves loincloths"* (v. 7 ESV).	**The God-fearing woman clothes herself in righteousness and is unafraid.** *"Strength and dignity are her clothing, and she laughs at the time to come"* (v. 25 ESV).
The fruit of Eve's hands was worthy of condemnation. *"Then the LORD God said to the woman, 'What is this that you have done?'"* (v. 13a ESV).	**The God-fearing woman bears good fruit worthy of praise.** *"Give her of the fruit of her hands, and let her works praise her in the gates"* (v. 31 ESV).

Proverbs 31 is a redemptive reversal of Genesis 3 in that the Proverbs 31 woman does what Eve failed to do—but this is not to say she "beats the curse" of sin. At best, she is what the book of Hebrews calls *"a shadow of the good things that are coming"* in Christ (Hebrews 10:1).

Jesus tells us, *"I am the vine; you are the branches. If you remain in me and I in you, you will bear much fruit"* (John 15:5).

CONCLUSION

To wrap up our Proverbs study and secure all we've learned of wise decision-making in our everyday lives, let's flip over to the New Testament to read a parable of Jesus—one that's all about invitations and therefore all about decisions.

Read Luke 14:1–24.

Every invitation requires a choice: Yes or no. Go or stay. And when a high-ranking Pharisee invited Jesus to dinner at his house in Luke 14:1, Jesus accepted. But by the end of the chapter, Jesus extended an invitation of His own, illustrating how those who love God follow a completely different decision-making logic than the rest of the world.

First, in verse 7, the Pharisees *"picked the places of honor"* for themselves around the dinner table, and Jesus responded with a parable emphasizing leadership through lowliness.

In Luke 14:13–14, who did Jesus tell the Pharisees to invite to banquets?

How does this connect to Proverbs 29:7?

Our study of Proverbs 31 discussed the trappings of comparing ourselves to others. How might this apply to the Pharisees' decision to rank themselves by social status (*"honor"*)?

"Blessed is the one who will eat at the feast of the kingdom of God!" exclaimed one Pharisee after hearing Jesus' parable (Luke 14:15). Here we might think, *Finally, they're getting it!* But it seems they had more

to learn. Verse 15 can also be translated, *"What a blessing it will be to attend a banquet in the Kingdom of God!"* (NLT), revealing the Pharisees' self-righteous assumption that they would sit at God's heavenly table in eternity . . . without accepting His invitation to trust in Christ on earth.

Unfortunately, that's not how God's invitation works. No one will feast in God's eternal Kingdom without having faith in His Son.

Jesus illustrated this truth in verses 16–24 through the parable of a banquet host (representing God) who invited many guests to a celebratory meal.

We see three reasons why people declined this invitation. Let's consider what motivated their choices:

DECISION	MOTIVATIONS
"I have just bought a field, and I must go and see it. Please excuse me." (Luke 14:18).	
"I have just bought five yoke of oxen, and I'm on my way to try them out. Please excuse me" (Luke 14:19).	
"I just got married, so I can't come" (Luke 14:20).	

Commentator David Guzik notes that refusing to attend the banquet was not the first mistake for the decision-makers in verses 18–19; both already had their priorities out of order since they made major purchases without even seeing what they were buying![1] The third decision-maker let the *immediate* matter of his marriage overshadow the *ultimate* matter of his eternity (God's banquet).

How does this echo what we learned from Proverbs 28:21 and Proverbs 14:4 about fixating on the immediate rather than the ultimate?

Jesus' parable turned out to be a prophecy about how the Pharisees would reject His invitation to eternal life because of their unbelief. The same is true for anyone who refuses to trust in Christ. Yet despite the earthly excuses of those who would reject Him, our great God has invited all the world—including gentiles (non-Jews), whom the Pharisees would have considered unclean—to follow Jesus and feast with Him forever (Luke 14:21–23).

Friend, that invitation is open to you and me. Jesus hand-delivered it by coming to earth, living a life of perfect obedience to God, dying on the cross to pay for all of our worst choices, and resurrecting in triumph over sin and death. Which means we have a decision to make.

So let's choose Jesus today. Then let's choose Him again tomorrow. Let's choose Him when it's hard and when it's easy and when we're lost and when we're hopeful and when we're tired and when we do the wrong thing and we need a second chance to choose again. At His table, *"there is still room"* (Luke 14:22).

To close our study, reread the invitation from Wisdom (whom many scholars associate with Jesus) in **Proverbs 8:32–35.** Choose a few words or phrases that stand out to you, and incorporate them into a prayer below.

FINAL REFLECTION & PRAYER

As we wrap up our study of Proverbs together, we pray the Lord has deepened your love for Him and your understanding of what it means to invite Him into your everyday decisions, from the major deliberations to the mundane moments and everything in between. Throughout this book of wisdom, we've seen so much evidence of God's faithfulness as a *"Wonderful Counselor"* (Isaiah 9:6) who offers loving guidance for every area of our lives.

Of course, that doesn't necessarily mean all our questions have been answered. Maybe you started this study on the verge of quitting your job, and you're still wondering if you should. Maybe you picked up this book hoping that through it, God would confirm where to send your kids to school, but the answer doesn't feel any clearer now than it did 31 days ago. Maybe you're even reconsidering decisions in your life that previously felt solid and certain, but Scripture has shifted your thinking.

Maybe that's right where God wants you, friend. Not in a place of insecure doubting but in a place of intentional dependence on Him.

Like Agur in Proverbs 30:8, you and I can bring all our unresolved questions to our Father and simply say, *"give me only my daily bread."* Or as Jesus puts it in the Lord's Prayer: *"Give us this day our daily bread"* (Matthew 6:11). God knows all our needs. However He chooses to meet them, we can trust Him to care for us as we commit our decisions and our hearts to Him.

So we keep praying. We keep seeking and keep asking. And we rest in the ultimate truth that no matter what job we have or where our kids go to school, our future is in good hands: *"Strength and dignity are [our] clothing,"* and we *"laugh at the time to come"* (Proverbs 31:25).

Lord, thank You for using Proverbs to encourage us in righteousness over the past 31 days—and thank You for drawing our attention to any unrighteous choices we need to leave behind to keep following You. Show us how to learn from the past, have faith in the present, and step confidently into the future Jesus secured for us on the cross. We choose not to get lost in the wilderness of worry and overthinking. We choose to trust You to lead us forward. In Jesus' name, amen.

NOTES

NOTES

ENDNOTES

Welcome Letter
1. "Proverbs," The Bible Project, May 31, 2016, https://bibleproject.com/explore/video/proverbs/.
2. Charles Bridges, *Proverbs: The Crossway Classic Commentaries* (Crossway Books, 2001), xiii.

How and to Where Our Decisions Lead Us: Jesus Is the Way
1. Robert Frost, "The Road Not Taken," in *Mountain Interval* (Henry Holt and Company, 1916).
2. Megan Marples, "Decision fatigue drains you of your energy to make thoughtful choices. Here's how to get it back," CNN, April 21, 2022, https://www.cnn.com/2022/04/21/health/decision-fatigue-solutions-wellness/index.html.
3. David Murray, "8 Lessons on Evangelism from Proverbs," Ligonier Ministries, February 9, 2023, https://www.ligonier.org/learn/articles/8-lessons-evangelism-proverbs.

Who Wrote Proverbs?
1. Duane A. Garrett, *Proverbs, Ecclesiastes, Song of Songs: An Exegetical and Theological Exposition of Holy Scripture,* vol. 14 of *The New American Commentary* (Broadman & Holman Publishers, 1993), 245.

Day 1
1. A. W. Tozer, *The Knowledge of the Holy* (HarperCollins, 1978), 1.

Day 2
1. Megan Sauter, "Dating the Copper Scroll," *Bible History Daily* (blog), Biblical Archaeology Society, April 17, 2025, https://www.biblicalarchaeology.org/daily/biblical-artifacts/dead-sea-scrolls/dating-the-copper-scroll/.

Day 5
1. Thomas Constable, DD, "Commentary on Proverbs 5:16," *Dr. Constable's Expository Notes*, StudyLight, https://www.studylight.org/commentaries/dcc/proverbs-5.html.

Day 7
1. Jon Simpson, "Finding Brand Success in the Digital World," *Forbes*, updated April 14, 2022, https://www.forbes.com/sites/forbesagencycouncil/2017/08/25/finding-brand-success-in-the-digital-world/?sh=2da3dc9f626e.
2. John Trapp, "Commentary on Proverbs 7," *Trapp's Complete Commentary*, StudyLight, https://www.studylight.org/commentaries/eng/jtc/proverbs-7.html.

Day 8
1. *ESV Study Bible* (Crossway, 2008), quoted in "Introduction to Proverbs," The Gospel Coalition, accessed April 21, 2026, https://www.thegospelcoalition.org/course/proverbs/#overview.
2. David Guzik, "Proverbs 8 – In Praise of Wisdom," The Enduring Word Bible Commentary, accessed April 21, 2026, https://enduringword.com/bible-commentary/proverbs-8/.

Day 9
1. Bible Hub, "Strong's Hebrew: 6612. פְּתִי (pthiy)," accessed April 21, 2026, https://biblehub.com/he-

brew/6612.htm.
2. Derek Kidner, *Proverbs*, quoted in David Guzik, "Proverbs 9 – Wisdom's Feast and Folly's Funeral," The Enduring Word Bible Commentary, https://enduringword.com/bible-commentary/proverbs-9/.

Day 10
1. Bruce K. Waltke and Ivan D. V. De Silva, *Proverbs: A Shorter Commentary* (William B. Eerdmans Publishing Company, 2021), 519.
2. Waltke and De Silva, *Proverbs*, 523.

Day 12
1. David Guzik, "Proverbs 12 – Words, Deeds, and Destiny," The Enduring Word Bible Commentary, https://enduringword.com/bible-commentary/proverbs-12/.
2. Bible Hub, "Strong's Hebrew: 5975. עָמַד (amad)," https://biblehub.com/hebrew/5975.htm.

Day 13
1. *ESV Study Bible* (Crossway, 2008), quoted in "Introduction to Proverbs," The Gospel Coalition, accessed April 21, 2026, https://www.thegospelcoalition.org/course/proverbs/#overview.

Day 14
1. Sinclair Ferguson, "What Is Discernment?" Ligonier Ministries, January 6, 2023, https://www.ligonier.org/learn/articles/discernment-thinking-gods-thoughts.

How Can I Trust My Own Discernment?
1. Jen Wilkin, *In His Image: 10 Ways God Calls Us to Reflect His Character*, (Crossway Books, 2018), 12.

Day 15
1. Waltke and De Silva, *Proverbs*, 676.

Day 16
1. Alicia Britt Chole, *Anonymous: Jesus' Hidden Years . . . and Yours* (Thomas Nelson, 2006).

Day 18
1. David Guzik, "Proverbs 18 – Wisdom in Getting Along with Others," The Enduring Word Bible Commentary, https://enduringword.com/bible-commentary/proverbs-18/.

Day 19
1. "What Does Proverbs 19:17 Mean?" BibleRef, accessed April 21, 2026, https://www.bibleref.com/Proverbs/19/Proverbs-19-17.html.
2. Avital Snow, "The Meaning of Hesed: Hebrew Word for Love," Fellowship of Israel Related Ministries, May 27, 2021, https://firmisrael.org/learn/the-meaning-of-hesed-hebrew-for-love/.

Day 22
1. "Prudence," Bible Hub, accessed April 21, 2026, https://biblehub.com/topical/p/prudence.htm.
2. Bible Hub, "Strong's Hebrew: 6175. עָר֫וּם (arum)," https://biblehub.com/hebrew/6175.htm.
3. Bible Hub, "pthiy."
4. Charles Bridges, *Proverbs,* Vol. 26, *The Crossway Classic Commentaries* (Crossway Books, 2001), 201.

Day 23
1. David Guzik, "Proverbs 23 – Words of the Wise" The Enduring Word Bible Commentary, https://enduringword.com/bible-commentary/proverbs-23/.
2. Bible Hub, "Strong's Hebrew: 309. אָחַר (achar)," https://biblehub.com/hebrew/309.htm.

Day 25
1. Nancy Guthrie, "What Not to Say to a Grieving Person," Crossway, October 19, 2016, https://www.crossway.org/articles/what-not-to-say-to-a-grieving-person/.

What's the Hurry?
1. "The Ten Symptoms of Hurry Sickness," New Ground Counseling, https://www.newgroundcounseling.com/blog/hurry-sickness.
2. Ann Voskamp, *One Thousand Gifts: A Dare to Live Fully Right Where You Are* (Thomas Nelson, 2011), 64.

Day 26
1. *Cambridge English Dictionary*, "trust," accessed April 21, 2026, https://dictionary.cambridge.org/us/dictionary/english/trust.
2. David Guzik, "Proverbs 26 – The Nature of the Fool and the Lazy Man," The Enduring Word Bible Commentary, https://enduringword.com/bible-commentary/proverbs-26/.

Day 27
1. Marshall Segal, "You Still Need Good Friends," Desiring God, July 29, 2022, https://www.desiringgod.org/articles/you-still-need-good-friends.
2. David Guzik, "Proverbs 27 – Planning for the Future, Receiving Honor," The Enduring Word Bible Commentary, https://enduringword.com/bible-commentary/proverbs-27/.

Day 29
1. Bible Hub, "Strong's Hebrew: 3045. יָדַע (yada)," https://biblehub.com/hebrew/3045.htm.
2. Lore Ferguson Wilbert, "Leadership Is Lonely (and It Should Be)," The Gospel Coalition, March 24, 2014, https://www.thegospelcoalition.org/article/leadership-is-lonely-and-it-should-be/.

Day 30
1. Waltke and De Silva, *Proverbs,* 1151–1158.
2. David Guzik, "Proverbs 30 – The Wisdom of Agur," The Enduring Word Bible Commentary, https://enduringword.com/bible-commentary/proverbs-30/.
3. Alex Kirk, "When Scripture Gets Weird: Understanding Agur in Proverbs 30," The Gospel Coalition, April 12, 2021, https://www.thegospelcoalition.org/article/agur-proverbs-30/.

Day 31
1. Adrien Segal, "Who Can Find Her? Rethinking the Proverbs 31 Standard," Desiring God, February 27, 2018, https://www.desiringgod.org/articles/who-can-find-her.
2. Waltke and De Silva, *Proverbs*, 1198.

Conclusion
1. David Guzik, "Luke 14 – Feasts and Invitations," The Enduring Word Bible Commentary, https://enduringword.com/bible-commentary/luke-14/.

ALSO AVAILABLE FROM

PROVERBS 31 MINISTRIES

40 DAYS THROUGH THE BIBLE

In this personal Bible study you will take a journey through the storyline of the Bible in 40 days so you can see major themes, how they are all connected, and what that means for us as we read the Bible today. Discover the eight major things humanity longs for and how Jesus fulfills all of them for us, and stop the endless cycle of seeking and searching for satisfaction and find the answers to your deepest longings.

30 DAYS WITH JESUS

In *30 Days with Jesus: Experiencing His Presence Throughout the Old and New Testaments*, authors Lysa TerKeurst and Dr. Joel Muddamalle will help you come to understand that Jesus isn't hiding from us; He's waiting to be seen by us. You will experience His presence every single day learning to look for Jesus with greater intentionality throughout your day.

30 DAYS OF PRAYER

This study is about uncomplicating your prayer life and how you communicate with God using the book of Psalms. Explore how thirty psalms offer insight and guidance into seeking joy, expressing gratitude, grappling with sorrow, or searching for answers. Through this study you will be reminded that God doesn't expect perfection when you come to Him. He just askes you to come.

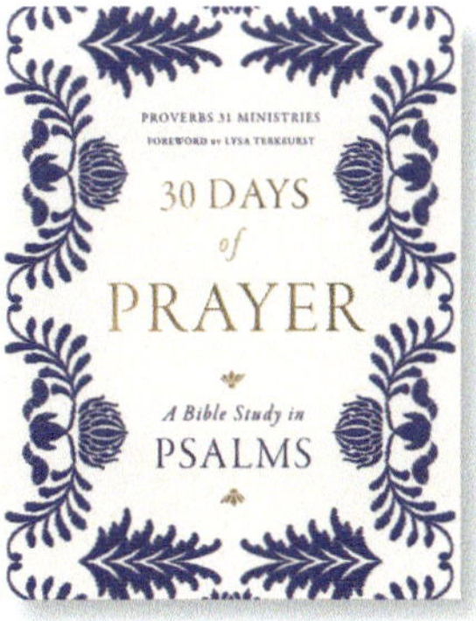

PROVERBS 31
ministries

Know the Truth. Live the Truth. It changes everything.

If you were inspired by this study and desire to deepen your own personal relationship with Jesus Christ, Proverbs 31 Ministries has just what you are looking for.

Proverbs 31 Ministries exists to be a trusted friend who will take you by the hand and walk by your side, leading you one step closer to the heart of God through:

- Online daily devotions
- First 5 Bible study app
- Therapy and Theology Podcast
- Proverbs 31 Ministries Podcast
- COMPEL Pro Writers Training
- She Speaks Conference
- Biblical books and resources

Our desire is to help you to know the Truth and live the Truth.
Because when you do, it changes everything.

For more information about Proverbs 31 Ministries, visit:
www.Proverbs31.org.

From the Publisher

GREAT STUDIES

ARE EVEN BETTER WHEN THEY'RE SHARED!

Help others find this study:

- Post a review at your favorite online bookseller
- Post a picture on a social media account and share why you enjoyed it
- Send a note to a friend who would also love it—or better yet, go through it with them

Thanks for helping others grow their faith!